BRAHMS STUDIES

VOLUME 1

Volume One

BRAHMS
Studies

Edited by

David Brodbeck

University of Nebraska Press

in affiliation with

the American Brahms Society

Lincoln and London

1994

CONTENTS

PREFACE

As these lines go to press, the American Brahms Society marks the first decade of its existence. Seeking to sustain the scholarly interest in Brahms's life, music, and historical position that had begun to swell in the period leading to the sesquicentennial of the composer's birth, in 1983, the Society's initial Board of Directors resolved to publish a series of *Brahms Studies*. The first of these volumes, edited by George S. Bozarth, appeared in 1990 and included all twenty-four papers that had been delivered at the International Brahms Conference held at the Library of Congress in Washington, D.C., in May 1983. The present volume, although more modestly scaled, is offered in the same spirit of providing a broad sampling of current Brahms research – which, as we rapidly approach the centennial of the composer's death, in 1997, remains in remarkably vigorous health.

Arranged chronologically by subject matter, the seven essays gathered here cover Brahms's entire career, from his early days in the Schumann household through the time of his final published work in the months before his death. The volume begins with George S. Bozarth's transcription and translation of Brahms's little-known collection of German proverbs, which the young composer set down in March 1855, and whose contents may offer one tool for making a fresh assessment of the youth's ethical and moral sensibilities. In David Brodbeck's examination of the exchange of counterpoint exercises that sprang up around this time between Brahms and his friend Joseph Joachim, we find evidence of Brahms's concern, not only to develop his compositional craft, but also to find expression of his troubled emotional entanglements with Robert and Clara Schumann. The greatest work to emerge from this period of study and emotional turmoil is the D-Minor Piano Concerto, the subject of a thoughtful analytical piece by Joseph Dubiel.

The long and productive middle phase of Brahms's career – running from the time of his "first maturity" in the early 1860s to his announcement, in 1890, of his intended retirement – is represented by two studies of the chamber music. John Daverio finds relevant precedents for one of Brahms's most characteristic *Mischformen*, not in Beethoven or Schubert (as has been supposed in the past), but in Mozart, who provided models that Brahms could appropriate in a "Romanticizing" gesture aimed at giving new life to sonata form. Margaret Notley combines a number of approaches – style-analytical, source study, *Rezeptionsgeschichte* – in her critical account of the Cello Sonata in F Major, op. 99, in which she relates certain peculiarities in style and structure to the unusual genesis of the work.

The final two essays concern works from Brahms's last period. In a study of the Intermezzo in E Minor, op. 119, no. 2, that has important implications for performance practice, Ira Braus argues, on the basis of both musical analysis and certain notational clues left in the score, that Brahms related the principal sections of the piece by means of what would later be termed a metrical modulation of 4 : 3. The volume concludes, fittingly enough, with an essay on the last of the works published during Brahms's lifetime, the *Vier ernste Gesänge*, op. 121. Here Daniel Beller-McKenna joins musical and textual analysis in an effort to place the songs in a larger cultural background; Brahms's choice, arrangement, and settings of these biblical texts, he suggests, can be read as the aging composer's affirmation of Romantic Idealism in the face of the Schopenhauerian pessimism that had been taken up by Wagner and other leading artists during the later nineteenth century.

Earlier versions of the essays by David Brodbeck, Joseph Dubiel, and John Daverio were presented, respectively, at the annual meeting of the American Musicological Society (Pittsburgh, November 1992) and the annual conference of the Royal Musical Association (Southampton, March 1993); the joint annual meeting of the American Musicological Society, the College Music Society, and the Society for Music Theory (Ann Arbor, Mich., 1982); and the Stanford Centennial Colloquium in Musicology ("Current Issues in the Interpretation of Mozart's Instrumental Music," Stanford University, May 1991). The essays by Margaret Notley and Daniel Beller-McKenna are derived from their recent Ph.D. dissertations, written at Yale and Harvard Universities, respectively, and completed with the support in part of the American Brahms Society's Karl Geiringer Scholarship in Brahms Studies.

Unless otherwise noted, all musical examples are based on the *Johannes Brahms Sämtliche Werke*, with the permission of Breitkopf & Härtel, Wiesbaden. Grateful acknowledgment is due to the Stadt- und Landesbibliothek, Vienna, for permission to publish the contents of Brahms's notebook of German proverbs and to the Staats- und Universitätsbibliothek Carl von Ossietzky, Hamburg, for permission to reproduce several leaves from the Nachlaß of Joseph Joachim.

Pittsburgh, May 1993   DB

ABBREVIATIONS

Billroth und Brahms   *Billroth und Brahms im Briefwechsel*, ed. Otto Gottlieb-Billroth (Berlin and Vienna: Urban & Schwarzenberg, 1935)

Brahms   *Brahms: Biographical, Documentary and Analytical Studies*, ed. Robert Pascall (Cambridge: Cambridge University Press, 1983)

Brahms 2   *Brahms 2: Biographical, Documentary and Analytical Studies*, ed. Michael Musgrave (Cambridge: Cambridge University Press, 1987)

Brahms Studies   *Brahms Studies: Analytical and Historical Perspectives*, ed. George S. Bozarth (Oxford: Clarendon Press, 1990)

Briefwechsel   *Johannes Brahms Briefwechsel*, 16 vols., rev. eds. (Berlin, 1912–22; reprint, Tutzing: Hans Schneider, 1974)

Briefwechsel, 3   *Johannes Brahms im Briefwechsel mit Karl Reinthaler, Max Bruch, Hermann Deiters, Friedr. Heimsoeth, Karl Reinecke, Ernst Rudorff, Bernhard und Luise Scholz*, ed. Wilhelm Altmann (2d ed., 1912)

Briefwechsel, 4   *Johannes Brahms im Briefwechsel mit J. O. Grimm*, ed. Richard Barth (1912)

Briefwechsel, 5–6   *Johannes Brahms im Briefwechsel mit Joseph Joachim*, ed. Andreas Moser, 2 vols. (vol. 1, 3d rev. ed., 1921; vol. 2, 2d rev. ed., 1912)

Briefwechsel, 8   *Briefe an Joseph Viktor Widmann, Ellen und Ferdinand Vetter, Adolf Schubring*, ed. Max Kalbeck (1915)

Briefwechsel, 9–10   *Johannes Brahms: Briefe an P. J. Simrock und Fritz Simrock*, ed. Max Kalbeck, 2 vols. (1917)

GdM   Gesellschaft der Musikfreunde, Vienna

Geiringer   Karl Geiringer, *Brahms: His Life and Works*, 3d ed. (New York: Da Capo Press, 1981)

Hofmann	Kurt Hofmann, *Die Bibliothek von Johannes Brahms* (Hamburg: Karl Dieter Wagner, 1974)
Joachim Nachlaß	Nachlaß J. Joachim, Staats- und Universitäts-bibliothek Carl von Ossietzky, Hamburg
Kalbeck, *Brahms*	Max Kalbeck, *Johannes Brahms*, rev. ed., 4 vols. in 8 (Berlin, 1915–21; reprint, Tutzing: Hans Schneider, 1976)
Litzmann, *Clara Schumann*	Berthold Litzmann, *Clara Schumann: Ein Künstlerleben nach Tagebüchern und Briefen*, 3 vols. (1902–8; reprint, Hildesheim: Georg Olms Verlag, 1971)
McCorkle	Margit L. McCorkle, *Johannes Brahms Thematisch-Bibliographisches Werkverzeichnis* (Munich: G. Henle Verlag, 1984)
Musgrave	Michael Musgrave, *The Music of Brahms* (London: Routledge & Kegan Paul, 1985)
Orel	Alfred Orel, "Ein eigenhändiges Werkverzeichnis von Johannes Brahms: Ein wichtiger Beitrag zur Brahmsforschung," *Die Musik* 29 (1937): 529–41
Schumann-Brahms Briefe	*Clara Schumann–Johannes Brahms: Briefe aus den Jahren 1853–1896*, ed. Berthold Litzmann, 2 vols. (1927; reprint, Hildesheim: Georg Olms Verlag; Wiesbaden: Breitkopf & Härtel, 1989)
Tovey, *Essays*, 3	Donald Francis Tovey, *Essays in Musical Analysis*, vol. 3, *Concertos* (London and New York: Oxford University Press, 1936)
Tovey, *Main Stream*	Donald Francis Tovey, *The Main Stream of Music and Other Essays* (New York and London: Oxford University Press, 1949)

ONE

Johannes Brahms's Collection of *Deutsche Sprichworte* (German Proverbs)

Edited and Translated by
George S. Bozarth

INTRODUCTION

In March 1855, while living in Düsseldorf near Clara Schumann and her children, Johannes Brahms filled a little commonplace book with German proverbs. This small, upright notebook, measuring 16.5 by 19.8 centimeters, was found in the composer's apartment after his death and acquired by the Wiener Brahms-Gesellschaft, which subsequently gave it, along with other Brahms documents, to the Handschriftensammlung of the Stadt- und Landesbibliothek in Vienna (catalog no. Ia 79.561).

Whether Brahms gathered these sayings together simply for his own enjoyment and edification or to be read by others as well – perhaps the Schumann children – we do not know. The notebook bears no dedication or other inscription that would provide a clue. The regular and spacious layout of the manuscript and the formality of title, date, and epigraph – "Good maxims, wise lessons one must practice, not just hear" – could suggest an intended readership of more than one. But Brahms was in the habit of preparing such compendiums for himself. In the early 1850s, he had filled several little notebooks with quotations from various poets, philosophers, writers, and musicians, entitling them the *Schatzkästlein des jungen Kreislers* (Little Treasure Chest of the Young

I would like to thank Susanne Vetter for her assistance with the initial transcription and translation of these proverbs, and Ben Kohn and Manfred Bansleben for their many valuable suggestions concerning the translations.

Kreisler), his nom de plume adopted from the fictional character Johannes Kreisler, the erratic Kapellmeister of E. T. A. Hoffmann's *Kreisleriana* and *Kater Murr.* These collections are well known in the Brahms literature, their contents having been published in 1909 by the Deutsche Brahms-Gesellschaft.[1] In comparison, Brahms's assemblage of German proverbs has been almost completely neglected, receiving only passing mention in Max Kalbeck's monumental biography of the composer.[2] Such a collection of everyday wisdom, though, tells much about the upbringing and beliefs of its compiler and is an important document for assessing the personality of the young Brahms.

Brahms's sources for the twenty-four proverbs copied on the first five pages of the collection are unknown. Thirteen of them were published in Karl Simrock's *Die deutschen Sprichwörter*, but eight others are not even to be found in Karl Friedrich Wilhelm Wander's comprehensive *Deutsche Sprichwörte-Lexicon*, a compendium drawing on hundreds of sources.[3] It is possible that Brahms's acquaintance with the proverbs in this first group stemmed from oral tradition rather than printed sources.

Brahms selected the rest of the proverbs, beginning with "Zeit gewonnen, viel gewonnen," from Karl Steiger's *Pretiosen deutscher Sprichwörter mit Variationen*. Indeed, his ordering follows Steiger's almost without exception.[4] Steiger organized his volume by the calendar year, with one

1. *Des jungen Kreislers Schatzkästlein, Aussprüche von Dichtern, Philosophen und Künstler,* zusammengetragen durch *Johannes Brahms*, ed. Carl Krebs (Berlin: Deutsche Brahms-Gesellschaft, 1909). This publication reproduces the contents of four small notebooks – two volumes of general quotations (the first begun in Hamburg in the late 1840s or early 1850s and completed in Düsseldorf in March 1854, the second begun directly thereafter) and two volumes devoted entirely to *Schöne Gedanken über Musik*, prepared in Düsseldorf and begun in September 1853 and July 1854, respectively. The volume begun in July 1854 is owned by the Handschriftensammlung of the Stadt- und Landesbibliothek (Ia 79.562); the identity of the present owners of the remaining volumes, once in the possession of Max Kalbeck, is unknown. (See George S. Bozarth, "Brahms's Lieder Inventory of 1859–60 and Other Documents of His Life and Work," *Fontes artis musicae* 30 [1983]: 108–9.) For additional remarks by various writers that Brahms marked in books in his library, see Karl Geiringer, "Brahms' zweites 'Schatzkästlein des jungen Kreisler,' " *Zeitschrift für Musik* 5 (1933): 443–46.

2. Kalbeck, *Brahms*, 1:182–83.

3. Karl Simrock, *Die deutschen Sprichwörter* (Frankfurt am Main: H. L. Brönner, 1846); Karl Friedrich Wilhelm Wander, *Deutsche Sprichwörte-Lexicon* (Leipzig: Brockhaus, 1867).

4. See Karl Steiger, *Pretiosen deutscher Sprichwörter mit Variationen* (St. Gallen: Scheitlin & Zollikofer, 1843). The proverbs, in the order in which Brahms copied them, are found in Steiger on pp. 3–6, 9, 10, 12–20, 28, 32, 37, 38, 41, 44–45, 57, 61, 71–73, 76, 77, 83–87, 103, 105,

proverb, together with its "variations" or prose elaborations, assigned to each day. In certain cases, the "variations" contain related proverbs, some of which Brahms also copied, at times linking them to the main proverb with a bracket.

In the following transcription, Brahms's distribution of the proverbs onto the pages of his notebook has been preserved. Words underlined by Brahms are printed in italic type; all editorial additions are placed in brackets, with the exception of apostrophes, which are supplied tacitly.[5]

110, 111, 113–18, 121, 122, 131, 132, 142, 144, 145, 151, 148, 151–62, 167–81, 183–95, 198–206, 209–11, 213, 217, 231, 237, 236, 239, 242, 243, 262, 267, 270–72, 466, and 487–88.

5. Brahms's continuing interest in the folk proverb is documented in three books from his library, each of which shows evidence of close scrutiny (annotations, underlining, etc.): Johann Agricola, *Siebenhundert und fünffzig Teutscher Sprüchworter* (1541; acquired by Brahms in 1895; GdM); Johann Gottlob Schulz, *Entstehung altdeutsche Sprüchwörter in kleinen Erzählungen vorgetragen* (Leipzig: Joh. Gottl. Imm. Breitkopf, 1793; Brahms-Institut, Lübeck [Sammlung Hofmann]); and *Wie das Volk spricht: Sprichwörtliche Redensarte*, 3d rev. ed. (Stuttgart: Adolph Krabbe, 1858; GdM). (See Hofmann, 110).

März 1855.

March 1855.

———

Gute Sprüche, weise Lehren
Muß man üben, nicht blos hören.

Good maxims, wise lessons
one must practice, not just hear.

———

2

Deutsche Sprichworte.
German Proverbs.

Wer Gott nicht hält,
Der fällt.

He who holds not with God,
will fall.

———

Das Herze ist das allerbest,
Das sich allzeit auf Gott verläßt.

That heart is the best of all
which always trusts in God.

———

Frisch und fröhlich zu seiner Zeit[,]
Fromm und treu in Ewigkeit.

Fresh and cheerful in the present,
pious and faithful in eternity.

———

Was du nicht willst, daß dir geschieht,
Das thu auch einem Andern nicht.

Do unto others as you would have them
do unto you.

———

3

———

Liebe pflanzt Liebe.

Love begets love.

———

Gedenke, daß, wo du auch bist,
Doch Gott in deiner Nähe ist.

Remember that wherever you are
God is close by.

———

Rede wenig, aber wahr,
Vieles Reden bringt Gefahr.

Speak little, but true;
too much talk is dangerous.

———

Junges Blut,
Spar dein Gut,
Armuth im Alter wehe thut.

Youth,
waste not;
poverty in old age is painful.

———

Pfau
schau
deine
Beine.

Peacock,
look to
your
legs.

———

4

———

Suchst du einen Thoren,
So fang' dich selbst bei den Ohren.

If you are looking for a fool,
seize yourself by the ears, *or*
To find a fool, start with yourself.

———

Die Alten zum Rath[,]
Die Jungen zur That.

The old for advice,
the young for action.

———

Wer's Alter nicht ehrt,
Ist des Alters nicht werth.

He who doesn't honor old age
isn't worthy of old age.

———

An Gottes Segen
Ist Alles gelegen.

Upon God's blessing
everything depends.

———

Merk auf die Stimme tief in dir;
Sie ist des Menschen Kleinod hier.

Heed the voice deep within yourself;
it is the jewel of mankind.

———

5

In Worten zart,
Zu Werken hart.

Gentle in words,
decisive in deeds.

Vergleichen und vertragen
Ist besser als zanken und klagen.

Compromising and getting along
is better than quarreling and complaining.

Aushorcher und Angeber
Sind des Teufels Netzeweber.

Meddlers and gossips
are weavers of the devil's nets.

Auf Rach
folgt Ach.

After revenge
follows regret.

Sanftmuth
Macht Alles gut.

Gentleness
sets everything right, *or*
A soft answer turneth away wrath.

6

———

Frisch begonnen
Halb gewonnen.

Well begun
half won.

———

Redlich sei des Herzens Grund,
Redlich spreche auch der Mund.

If your heart be honest,
your mouth will be too.

———

Iß, was gar ist,
Trink, was klar ist,
Sprich, was wahr ist.

Eat what is well-done,
drink what is clear,
speak what is true.

———

Reiner Mund und treue Hand
Gehen durch das ganze Land.

Honesty and fidelity
will get you through life.

———

Halt dich rein,
Acht dich klein,
Sei gern allein,
Mit Gott gemein.

Keep yourself pure,
be humble,
enjoy being alone,
at one with God.

———

7

———

Zeit gewonnen, viel gewonnen.

Time won, much won.

———

Der Fleißige hat immer was zu thun.

The diligent always has something to do.

———

Mit Fragen kommt man nach Rom.

Questioning leads one to Rome.

———

Fallen ist keine Schande, aber nicht wieder aufstehen.

Falling down is no disgrace, but not standing up again is.

———

Wer nichts Gutes thut, thut schon Böses genug.

He who does no good, does evil enough.

———

Wer flieht, der wird gejagt.

He who flees, will be hunted.

———

Der Geizige ist so dumm, wie Salomons Esel.

The stingy man is as stupid as Solomon's ass.

———

8

———

Gott gibt wohl die Kuh,
Aber nicht auch das Seil dazu.

God does provide the cow,
but not the rope to go with it, *or*
God helps those who help themselves.

———

Es gibt uns Gott wohl den Verstand
Doch Jeder nehm' ihn selbst zur Hand.

God does give us intelligence,
yet each person must set about using it himself.

———

Die Hausfrau muß nicht sein eine Ausfrau.

The wife must not wander.

———

Aus lauter Liebe frißt der Wolf das Schaf.

The wolf eats the sheep out of pure love.

———

Der Hehler ist so schlimm als der Stehler.

The fence is as bad as the thief.

———

Wer auf der Eb'ne bleibt,
fällt nicht tief. [Brahms:] (Freilich –)

He who stays on the plain,
will not fall far. [Brahms:] (Quite so –)

———

9

———

Wer auf ein Knie kommt, den stößt
man gern um; fällt er auf beide,
so haut man ihm den Kopf ab.

He who comes on one knee, one likes
to knock down; if he falls on both knees,
then one cuts off his head.

———

Wer an's Kreuz kommt, den tränkt man mit Essig und Galle.

He who is persecuted, is given vinegar and gall to drink.

———

Wer ein Ding nicht sehen will,
Dem hilft weder Aug' noch Brill'.

He who doesn't want to see something
is helped by neither eyes nor glasses.

———

Ein gut Gewissen
ist ein sanftes Ruhekissen.

A good conscience is a soft pillow, *or*
A good conscience makes a sound sleeper.

———

(Chinesisches Gnome.)

Sein Gewissen der Leidenschaft opfern, das heißt ein Bild
(ein Kunstwerk) verbrennen, um dessen Asche zu bekommen.

(Chinese Maxim.)

To sacrifice one's conscience to passion
is to burn a painting (a work of art) for its ashes.

———

10

———

Angesicht – die That ausspricht.

Face – the deed expressed, *or*
The face reveals all.

———

Des Jünglings Gesicht
Ist ein Gedicht.
In Mannes Gesichte
Lies seine Geschichte.

The youth's face
is a poem.
In a man's face
one reads his story.

———

Von Funken brennt das Haus.

A house in flames starts with sparks.

———

Ist eine Mutter noch so arm,
So gibt sie ihrem Kindt doch warm.

No matter how poor a mother is,
she still will keep her child warm.

———

Die Muttertreu'
ist täglich neu.

A mother's devotion
is renewed every day.

———

11

{13}

———

In Wein und Bier ertrinken mehr als in Wasser.

More drown in wine and beer than in water, *or*
Wine hath drowned more men than the sea.

———

Es trinken sich *Tausende* den Tod
Eh *Einer* stirbt in Durstes Noth.

Thousands die of drinking
before *one* dies of thirst.

———

Das Kreuz gefaßt,
ist halbe Last.

Taking up the cross
is half the burden.

———

Man sieht an die Leute hin,
aber nicht in die Leute hinein.

One looks *at* people,
but not *into* people.

———

Garn stellen fängt nicht Vögel, sondern zuziehen.

Setting a trap catches no birds, but pulling it shut does.

———

Laster, die man nicht tadelt, die säet man.

Vices not censured are sown.

———

12

―――

Wer der Leiter hinauf will,
muß bei der untersten Sprosse anfangen.

He who wants to climb a ladder,
must start with the bottom rung.

―――

Was soll der Kuh eine Muskatnuß? –
Es thut ihr genug ein Löcklein Heu.

What is the cow to do with a nutmeg? –
A curl of hay is enough for her, *or*
Why cast pearls to swine?

―――

Arm ist nicht wer wenig hat,
sondern wer viel bedarf.

He who has little is not poor,
but he who desires a lot is.

―――

Wer langsam reitet, soll früher satteln.

He who rides slowly, should saddle up earlier.

―――

Wo es eben geht ist gut Fuhrmann sein.

Where it is level, it is good to be a wagon driver.

―――

Genug ist besser als zuviel.

Enough is better than too much.

―――

13

———

Es ist eine Sache eher zerbrochen als gebaut.

A thing is more easily broken to pieces than put together.

———

Ein alter Baum ist schwer zu ver[p]flanzen.

An old tree is hard to transplant, *or*
You can't teach an old dog new tricks.

———

Fleiß bricht Eis.

Diligence breaks ice.

———

Wer nichts an Angel steckt, der wird nichts fahen.

He who puts nothing on the hook, will catch nothing.

———

Es ist einem Hund leid, wenn ein ander[er] in die Küche geht.

A dog doesn't like it when someone else goes into the kitchen.

———

Wenn's Kalb ertrunken ist, deckt man den Brunnen.

When the calf is drowned, one covers the well.

———

Wenn der Beutel leer ist, denkt man an's Sparen.

When the purse is empty, one thinks of saving.

———

14

———

Kein Kleid steht einer Frau besser, als Schweigen.

No dress is more becoming to a woman than silence.

———

Man muß das Bäumchen biegen, dieweil es noch jung ist.

One must bend the little tree while it's still young.

———

Reu
Des Herzens Arznei.

Repentance
The heart's medicine.

———

Wohl gebetet ist halb studirt.

Well prayed is half studied.

———

Jede Lüge will zehn andere zum Futter haben.

Every lie will have ten others as fodder, *or*
Lying is a slippery slope.

———

Wünscher und Woller sind schlechte Haushalter.

Wishes and wantings are bad housekeepers.

———

Eine Schwalbe macht noch keinen Sommer.

One swallow does not a summer make.

———

15

———

Wünscher und Woller
sind schlechte Haushalter.

Wishes and wantings
are bad housekeepers.

———

Es ist kein Räuchlein,
es ist auch ein Feuerlein.

Where there's a little smoke,
there's a little fire.

———

Tugend wächst im Unglück.

Virtue grows in misfortune, *or*
Suffering builds character.

———

Einen zeitigen Dieb erläuft
ein hinkender Scherg.

A lame constable
catches a punctual thief.

———

Gott macht genesen
Und der Arzt holt die Spesen.

God makes one well
and the doctor collects the fee.

———

16

———

Liebe deinen Nachbar –
reiße aber den Zaun nicht ein.

Love thy neighbor –
but don't tear down the fence.

———

Alter schützt vor Thorheit nicht.

Old age is no shield against folly.

———

Wer gegessen hat,
meint Andere seien auch satt.

He who has eaten,
believes others are full too.

———

Ueberall geht die Sonne Morgens auf.

The sun rises everywhere in the morning.

———

Wo viel Geld ist, da wohnet der Teufel,
wo aber keines ist, da sind zwei.

Where there's a lot of money, the devil dwells;
but where there's no money, there are two.

———

17

———

Man kann auf keinem Kissen
in den Himmel rutschen.

One cannot slide into heaven
on a pillow.

———

So man einem den Finger beut,
will er die ganze Hand.

If you offer someone a finger, he'll want your whole hand, *or*
Give him an inch and he'll take a mile.

———

Gott hilft dem Stärksten.

God helps the strongest.

———

Durch Schaden wird man klug.

Through injury one becomes prudent, *or*
Once bitten, twice shy.

———

Es gehen viele geduldige Schäflein in einen Stall.

Many patient little sheep fit into a stall.

———

Was eines Andern ist,
Darnach man hat Gelüst.

One longs for what belongs to another, *or*
The grass is always greener on the other side of the fence.

———

18

———

Morgenstund
hat Gold im Mund.

Morning is the golden time, *or*
An hour in the morning is worth two in the evening, *or*
The early bird catches the worm.

———

Putzen wollen Alle den Docht,
aber ihm Oel zugießen Keiner.

Everyone wants to clean the wick,
but no one wants to fill up the oil.

———

Das Glück ist kugelrund.

Luck is round as a ball.

———

Was hilft ein goldener Fingerring
wider den Wurm am Nagel.

What good is a golden ring on the finger
against inflammation under the nail, *or*
Wealth is no guarantee against suffering.

———

Die Letzten werden die Ersten sein.

The last shall be the first.

———

19

———

Thue Recht
und scheue Niemand!

Act justly
and fear no one!

———

Man muß nicht mit der Thür[e] in's Haus fallen.

One needn't burst into the house when the door's open.

———

Wem das Wasser in's Maul geht,
der lernt schwimmen.

He who gets water in his mouth,
learns how to swim, *or*
Necessity is the mother of invention.

———

Besser Mann ohne Geld, als Geld ohne Mann.

Better a husband without money than money without a husband.

———

Der Unschuldige muß Viel leiden.

The innocent must suffer much.

———

Lob ist der Thoren Prob'.

Praise is the fool's test.

———

20

———

Warten – ist immer zu früh.

Waiting – is always too early.

———

Wer sich auf's Erben verlot
Kommt z'früh oder z'spot.

He who counts on his inheritance,
comes too early or too late.

———

Undank ist der Welt Lohn.

Ingratitude is the world's reward.

———

Wein ein, Witz aus.

Wine in, wit out.

———

Voll – toll.

Full [of wine] – crazy.

———

Trunk'ne Freud, nüchtern Leid.

Drunken joy, sober sorrow.

———

Süß getrunken, sauer bezahlt.

Sweetly drunk, sour paid, *or*
After sweet meat comes sour sauce.

———

21

―――

Tugend ist der beste Adel.

Virtue is the highest nobility.

―――

Der Ehre gebührt ein Thron[,]
nicht Ehre dem Thron.

It is honor that deserves a throne,
not the throne that deserves honor.

―――

Wer die Augen nicht aufthut,
muß den Beutel aufthun.

He who does not open his eyes,
must open his wallet.

―――

Gezwung'ne Eh' –
des Herzens Weh.

Forced marriage –
the heart's woe.

―――

Keine Regel ohne Ausnahme.

No rule without exceptions.

―――

Alte Leute sehen am besten in die Ferne.

Old people are the best at seeing the large picture.

―――

22

———

Wer viel redet, lügt viel.

He who talks a lot, lies a lot.

———

Mit Zeit und Geduld wird
aus der Hanfstengel ein Halskragen.

With time and patience
a strand of hemp can become a nice collar.

———

Die Liebe muß gezankt haben.

Love must have quarreling.

———

Willst du dich deines Werths erfreu'n,
Mußt du der Welt auch Werth verleih'n.

If you want to take pleasure in your worth,
you must also bestow your worth on the world.

———

Wer schimpft,
der hat verloren.

He who insults,
has lost.

———

23

———

Aufschieb
ist ein Tagdieb.

A postponer
is an idler.

———

Aufgeschoben
ist nicht aufgehoben.

Postponed is not canceled, *or*
All is not lost, that is delayed.

———

(Vertagt ist nicht geleistet.)

(Adjourned is not achieved.)

———

Es hinkt Keiner an eines Andern Fuß.

No one limps with another's foot.

———

Will man dir übel, so bricht man Hader ab dem Zaun.

If someone wishes you ill, he will pick a quarrel.

———

Der Feinde Fehler soll man kennen,
aber nicht nennen.

One should know the faults of one's enemies,
but not speak of them.

———

24

———

Wer nicht will sein betrogen,
Der kauf' des Nachbars Rind
Und freie dessen Kind.

He who wishes not to be deceived,
will buy his neighbor's cow
and marry his neighbor's daughter.

———

Dein Herz dein Rath.

Your heart, your advice, *or*
Follow your heart.

———

Wer Gott vertraut,
hat wohl gebaut.

He who trusts in God,
has built well.

———

Alte Freunde und alten Wein
muß man zusammenhalten.

Old friends and old wine
must be treasured.

———

25

———

Dem Reinen ist Alles rein.

To the pure, everything is pure.

———

Es liegt nicht immer am Wohlspielen,
sondern auch am Gernhören.

It's not always the good playing,
but also liking to listen.

———

In ander[er] Leute Garten ist gut grasen.

In other people's gardens the grazing is good, *or*
The grass is greener on the other side of the fence.

———

Vom Verräther frißt kein Rabe.

No raven will feed on a traitor.

———

Gerade heraus ist Meister.

Frankness is master.

———

26

———

Wenn Falschheit brennete als Feuer,
So wäre das Holz nicht halb so theuer.

If lies could burn,
firewood would be cheap.

———

Gute Vorsätze sind ein gepflasterter Weg zur Hölle.

Good intentions are a paved road to hell.

[A variant of:

Der Weg zur Hölle ist mit guten Vorsätzen gepflastert.

The way to hell is paved with good intentions.]

———

27

TWO

The Brahms-Joachim
Counterpoint Exchange;
or, Robert, Clara, and "the
Best Harmony between
Jos. and Joh."

David Brodbeck

You ask for news of Brahms; all is very well with him, I am certain, for he must be feeling aware of his inner riches. Just lately he sent me some work, among which was a Fugue for Organ that combines depth and tenderness of feeling with a wealth of musical art so nobly that even Bach and Beethoven have scarcely excelled it. . . . So poor Schumann with his enthusiasm was braver than any of those who laughed at his prophetic airs. – Letter of Joseph Joachim to Gisela von Arnim, 20 June 1856[1]

The fits and starts by which Johannes Brahms began his professional career are well known. In barely seven months' time following the electrifying appearance, in October 1853, of Robert Schumann's prophetic essay "Neue Bahnen," he brought out his first eight opera, including the recently composed Piano Sonata in F Minor and Piano Trio in B Major, as well as other piano works and songs dating

I wish to thank Professors George S. Bozarth, Walter Frisch, and William Little for their helpful comments. Generous financial support was provided by a grant from the Faculty of Arts and Sciences, University of Pittsburgh.

1. *Briefe von und an Joseph Joachim* (hereafter *Joachim Briefe*), ed. Johannes Joachim and Andreas Moser, 3 vols. (Berlin, 1911–13), 1:351; translated in *The Musician's World: Letters of the Great Composers*, ed. Hans Gal (London: Thames & Hudson, 1965), 304.

back to as early as 1851. Then, in the summer of 1854, he completed two important new works for piano – the "Schumann" Variations and the Four Ballades, both of which soon also appeared in print. But after this promising start, silence: no new composition was published until December 1860. Brahms was not idle, of course. In 1854–55, he wrestled with an aborted Duo Sonata-Symphony in D Minor and in the following year worked, with somewhat greater success, on a Piano Quartet in C♯ Minor.[2] Yet, under the twin pressures of Schumann's high public praise and his own exacting self-criticism, Brahms knew that he was overreaching in these ambitious new works. As he put it to Clara Schumann in a wistful letter of 12 February 1856: "It always saddens me that I am still not a proper musician, but I have talent for it, more, probably, than is usual in young people nowadays. It gets driven out of you. Boys should be allowed to make jolly music; the serious kind comes soon enough by itself; only the lovesick-type [*Schmachtlappige*] doesn't. How lucky is the man who, like Mozart and others, arrives at the tavern in the evening and writes new music. He lives only for his creating but does what he wants. What a man."[3]

Brahms understood that he was no Mozart, much less, to borrow a colorful metaphor from "Neue Bahnen," the "young blood" who "would not gain his mastery by gradual stages" but "spring fully armed like Athena from the head of Zeus." He knew otherwise and, indeed, soon embarked on a rigorous program of musical education involving the exchange of difficult assignments in traditional counterpoint with his friend Joseph Joachim. Not surprisingly, this "correspondence course" saw the creation of a good deal of music of the "serious kind." But, as we shall discover, some rather "lovesick" work came of it, too.

---

2. Among other studies, see Christopher Reynolds, "A Choral Symphony by Brahms?" *19th-Century Music* 9 (1985): 3–25; George S. Bozarth, "Brahms's First Piano Concerto, Op. 15: Genesis and Meaning," in *Beiträge zur Geschichte des Konzerts: Festschrift Siegfried Kross zum 60. Geburtstag,* ed. Reinmar Emans and Matthias Wendt (Bonn: Gundrum Schröder Verlag, 1990), 211–47; and James Webster, "The C Sharp Minor Version of Brahms's Op. 60," *Musical Times* 121 (1980): 89–93. The beginnings of the quartet seem to date from 1855; see Clara Schumann's reference in her letter to Joseph Joachim of 28 March 1855 to "einem herrlichen ersten Pianoforte Quartett-Satz" (quoted in Renate Hofmann, "Johannes Brahms im Spiegel der Korrespondenz Clara Schumanns," in *Brahms und seine Zeit: Symposium Hamburg 1983,* ed. Constantin Floros, Hans Joachim Marx, and Peter Petersen [Laaber: Laaber Verlag, 1984], 48).

3. Litzmann, *Clara Schumann,* 2:404. Unless otherwise noted, all translations are mine.

I

From his first days in Düsseldorf, following Robert Schumann's suicide attempt in February 1854, the young Brahms occupied himself with the study of early music. In April of that year, using the rich resources of the Schumann library, he copied two works that were thought to be by Palestrina and, at about the same time, applied himself to the art of canon.[4] By the beginning of February 1855, now boasting of an ability to produce canons "in all possible artistic forms," he expressed an interest in composing fugues.[5] Then, six weeks later, he invited Clara Schumann to become a partner in his plan to "pass the time . . . with counterpoint!"[6]

4. The "Palestrina" works are in fact by Ingegneri. Brahms's copies (dated "Ddf. April 54") are found among many others that he made of Renaissance and Baroque pieces during the years 1854–60; this miscellany is preserved in the composer's estate (GdM, A134) and registered in McCorkle as Anh. Va, Nr. 7. The guide to Brahms's canon studies seems to have been J. A. André's *Lehrbuch der Tonsetzkunst* (1838–40), from which, using paper identical to that which he had used in making the Ingegneri copies, Brahms transcribed several intricate examples by J. S. Bach, Mozart, William Byrd, and André himself. This copy forms the first leaf in a miscellany containing copies that Brahms made over many years of canons drawn from a wide variety of sources. This collection likewise is preserved in the composer's estate (GdM, A131) and is registered in McCorkle as Anh. Va, Nr. 5. (See also Virginia Hancock, *Brahms's Choral Compositions and His Library of Early Music* [Ann Arbor, Mich.: UMI Research Press, 1983], 37, 47–48.) The first fruits of Brahms's canon study may be seen in nos. 8, 10, 14, and 15 of the "Schumann" Variations. Other works that might stem from this time include the two-part retrograde canon "In dieser Welt des Trugs," WoO posthum 27, and perhaps even nos. 1, 8, and 10–12 of the Thirteen Canons, op. 113 (which, in any case, are found among the collection of parts that Brahms used in 1859–62, when he conducted his *Hamburger Frauenchor*). For a brief survey of Brahms's self-contained canonic pieces, see Siegfried Kross, "Brahms und der Kanon," in *Festschrift Joseph Schmidt-Görg zum 60. Geburtstag*, ed. Dagmar Weise (Bonn: Beethoven Haus, 1957), 175–87.

5. See Brahms's letter to Clara Schumann of 3 February 1855: "I can now make canons in all possible artistic forms; I'm eager [to see] how I'll do with fugues again" (*Schumann-Brahms Briefe*, 1:73). Brahms's appetite for fugue must have been whetted by his recent experience of composing, in January 1855, the Gigues in A Minor and B Minor, WoO 4, both of which show the traditional imitative style of Baroque models. In a diary entry of 12 February 1856, Clara noted that "Johannes played me canons and gigues of his; he can do anything he wants" (Litzmann, *Clara Schumann*, 2:366). (See also William Horne, "Brahms's Düsseldorf Suite Study and His Intermezzo, Opus 116, No. 2," *Musical Quarterly* 73 [1989]: 249–83.)

6. *Schumann-Brahms Briefe*, 1:100. Compare the epigraph that Brahms chose for the collection of German proverbs that he made at about the same time: "Good maxims, wise lessons one must practice, not just hear." That many of the proverbs in Brahms's gathering affirm a traditional "work ethic" is quite in keeping with the personality of a composer who wished to

Although Frau Schumann soon recorded in her diary that she had "begun theoretical studies with Johannes,"[7] little came of this joint project, and Brahms was left to continue his self-tuition. During the winter of 1855–56, he acquired a number of significant theoretical treatises, including the portions of Kirnberger's *Die Kunst des reinen Satzes in der Musik* dealing with double counterpoint, a rare first edition of Mattheson's *Der vollkommene Capellmeister*, and Simon Sechter's 1843 edition of Marpurg's *Abhandlung von der Fuge.*[8] Finally, on 26 February 1856, Brahms invited Joachim to join his studies, proposing a weekly exchange of contrapuntal exercises that might be continued until both men had become "quite adept." After all, Brahms added, "Why shouldn't we two quite reasonable and serious people be able to teach ourselves – and much better than some professor could?"[9] This letter

---

retreat from the glare of publicity raised by "Neue Bahnen" in order to develop his craft. Most telling is the proverb "He who stands on the plain will not fall far," which drew Brahms's wholehearted assent, as indicated by his annotation "Quite so – ." (See Bozarth, in this volume.)

7. Litzmann, *Clara Schumann*, 2:370.

8. The Kirnberger was among several books that Brahms purchased in November 1855, during enchanted hours spent in the secondhand bookshops of Hamburg; the Mattheson and Marpurg – which Brahms had sought but was unable to find there – were received as gifts from, respectively, Joachim (for Christmas 1855) and Clara (in January 1856). See Brahms's letter to Frau Schumann of 28 November 1855: "I spend literally half the day here at antiquarian shops, yet I certainly don't consider the time to be wasted; the searching is well rewarded by the finding. But unfortunately I still haven't found any book by Mattheson nor the best by Marpurg: the one about fugue. But how many other beautiful and important ones" (*Brahms-Schumann Briefe*, 1:154). See also Brahms's letter of 30 November: "Think of my joy: Avé has a large floor full of unordered music, the most magnificent things, I often rummage about there, and I'm able to take duplicates [*Doubletten*] with me. I won't write any more to you [about] what new and magnificent things I've found but rather will look forward to the happy hour in Düsseldorf when I can show you everything" (ibid., 156). For a fuller account of the early music materials that Brahms acquired at this time, see Hancock, *Brahms's Library of Early Music*, 72–78. Brahms seems to have gone right to work on the Kirnberger, which included the author's solutions to the canons in Bach's *Musikalisches Opfer*; in a letter to Clara of 8 December 1855 (*Schumann-Brahms Briefe*, 1:158), he noted a reminiscence of Bach's piece in the "beautiful Adagio" of Robert Schumann's Second Symphony. As Linda Correll Roesner has noted, the main theme of Schumann's slow movement recalls the opening of the Largo of Bach's *Sonata sopr'il soggetto reale* (see "Tonal Strategy and Poetic Content in Schumann's C-Major Symphony, Op. 61," in *Probleme der symphonischen Tradition im 19. Jahrhundert*, ed. Siegfried Kross with Marie Luise Maintz [Tutzing: Hans Schneider, 1990], 299n).

9. *Briefwechsel*, 5:123–24. On 27 February 1856, Joachim reported to Clara Schumann, "Yes-

marks the beginning of an extensive "musical correspondence," the progress of which may be followed in table 2.1.

Although Joachim immediately agreed to Brahms's proposition, he was too busy to settle down to work straightaway. The first step, therefore, was made by Brahms, who toward the end of March sent his friend "zwei kleine Stücke," which can be identified, as we shall see, as a four-voice Benedictus and an augmentation canon in five parts (see table 2.1, item 1). At the same time, hoping to spur Joachim to action, Brahms formalized the rules that were to govern the exchange, including the imposition of a friendly fine of one taler, to be used for buying books, when work was not forwarded in a timely manner.[10]

In spite of this encouragement – and perhaps intimidated by Brahms's example – Joachim did not send his first studies until late April. But for three months thereafter the exchange continued productively. To Joa-

---

terday I had the most friendly news from Johannes, who proposes a contrapuntal exchange . . . [that] promises the best harmony between Jos. and Joh.; if eventually . . . you join in, it will not be lacking its most beautiful measure!" (*Joachim Briefe*, 1:319).

10. "I am enclosing two little pieces as a beginning of our joint studies. Should you have a mind for the thing, then I'd like to lay down some rules that I find useful. Every Sunday exercises [*Arbeiten*] must go back and forth. On one Sunday, for example, you send [something], on the next I return the exercise with one of my own, and so forth. But whoever misses the day, that is, sends nothing, must instead send one taler, which the other can use to buy books!!! Only if instead of an exercise ones sends a composition is he excused. . . . Will you join in? In that case, send the [two] pieces back to me next Sunday . . . , along with others [of your own]. Double counterpoint, canons, fugues, preludes, or whatever it may be." Letter of ca. 24 March 1856, in *Briefwechsel*, 5:126–27. My identification of the two unnamed studies hinges on Joachim's subsequent evaluation of the works, which I discuss below. Brahms's "rules" give evidence of his remarkably intimate acquaintance with the private lives of Robert and Clara Schumann; indeed, the lines in question read like a paraphrase of the following delightful passage from Robert's initial entry in the first of the couple's so-called marriage diaries (from 1840–41): "Once a week we will trade the secretarial duties, exchanging the diary every Sunday (early, at coffee time, if possible) so that nobody can be kept from also adding a kiss. . . . The recording of one week may never amount to less than a single page; whoever fails in this respect shall receive some sort of punishment, which we will have to figure out. Should it occur to one member of our marital team not to turn anything in for a whole week, then the penalty will be made very much harsher – an almost unimaginable circumstance, considering our well-known mutual high esteem and sense of duty" (*The Marriage Diaries of Robert & Clara Schumann*, ed. Gerd Nauhaus, trans. Peter Ostwald [Boston: Northeastern University Press, 1993], 3–4). The possibility raised here that Brahms might have read the diaries – during his Düsseldorf years, after all, he had the run of the Schumanns' apartment – is but one of several indications, as we shall see, that in the joint contrapuntal studies with Joachim he sought to identify personally with Schumann.

Table 2.1. Brahms-Joachim *Notenkorrespondenz*, February–July 1856

Date of Letter[a]	From	Work Submitted	Work Criticized; Other Remarks
26 Feb 56 (90)	Brahms		Formally proposes the counterpoint exchange
3 Mar 56 (91)	Joachim		Agrees to Brahms's proposal
21 Mar 56 (92)	Joachim		Signed "Dein unkontrapunktischer J.J."
24 Mar 56 (93)	Brahms	1. 4-voice canonic setting of Benedictus (WoO 18); 5-voice augmentation canon (op. 29/2)	Proposes rules to govern exchange
20 Apr 56 (96)	Joachim	2. Fugue subjects/answers on B–A–C–H; fugal passage for string quartet	
22 Apr 56 (97)	Joachim	3. Unresolved 2-voice inversion canon on F–A– E/ Gis–E–La; 2-voice canon over free bass in F major; E–A–F fugue subject and answer	Returns item 1 without comment
24 Apr 56 (98)	Joachim	4. Unresolved 2-voice circle canon (lost but transcribed in *Bw*, 5:133)	
27 Apr 56 (100)	Brahms	5. 2-voice circle canon on revised subject of item 4 (Anh. III, Nr. 3); item 1 resubmitted for review; several canons in C minor for strings, including one 4- voice circle canon (lost); several canonic imitations on subject of Bach's *Art of Fugue* (lost)	Comments on items 2–4; sets Joachim the task of writing additional canons on *Art of Fugue* subject

a. All references are to *Briefwechsel*, 5 (3d rev. ed.). Italic type indicates that the date has been supplied. The number given in parentheses is the number assigned to the letter in this edition.

30 Apr 56 (101)	Joachim	6. 2-voice canon over F–A–E / Gis–E–La bass; 7-voice double canon ("Schulfuchserei"); 2-voice canon set over an Irish *Elfenlied*; 3-voice canon set under the Irish *Elfenlied*; variation on the Irish *Elfenlied* (lost)	
4 May *56* (102)	Joachim	7. Eight 2-voice canons over *Art of Fugue* subject	Mentions a "good, short" fugue subject that is to be worked out soon (probably a reference to the 3-voice fugue using the F–A–E canon subject of item 3 that is preserved in the Joachim Nachlaß but that Brahms apparently never saw); includes payment of "fine" and promises to comment on Brahms's work soon. Intended to return Brahms's work but arrived too late at the post office
31 May *56* (103)	Joachim		
1 *Jun 56* (104)	Joachim	8. Eight two-voice canons with one free voice?	Finally comments on items 1 and 5
5 *Jun 56* (105)	Brahms	9. Prelude and Fugue in A Minor, WoO 9; Fugue in A♭ Minor, WoO 8; *Geistliches Lied*, op. 30	Comments on items 6 and 7
16 Jun *56* (106)	Joachim	10. Two canons over *Art of Fugue* subject (lost); 2-voice canon over the Irish *Elfenlied* and free bass for string quartet; *Uebungen in der Variation-Form* (i.e., the Irish *Elfenlied* and several variations for piano) (only partially preserved)	Comments on item 9

22 Jun 56 (107)	Brahms	11. Kyrie, WoO 17; Sanctus, Osanna, Agnus Dei, WoO 18; two "innocent canonic melodies" (unresolved versions of op. 37/1–2)	Comments on item 10
Jul 56 (109)	Joachim	12. Revision and extension of the variation set on the Irish *Elfenlied* (now called simply *Variationen*)[b]	Promises to comment soon on item 11
Jul 56 (108)	Joachim		Comments on Mass movements submitted in item 11; makes no comment on the "innocent canonic melodies"
22 Jul 56 (110)	Brahms		Comments on item 12; mentions a "half-finished" Credo

b. The first edition of this set, edited by Michael Struck, has recently appeared as *Variationen über ein irisches Elfenlied* (Hamburg: J. Schuberth, 1989).

chim's credit may be counted a number of fugue subjects with their answers (including several on the notes B–A–C–H), a wide variety of little canons (including some, as assigned by Brahms, worked out over the subject of Bach's *Art of Fugue*), and a set of variations for piano on an Irish *Elfenlied* (see table 2.1, items 2–4, 6–8, 10, and 12). Brahms's contributions were even more substantial: in addition to the Benedictus setting and augmentation canon, we find evidence of several lost canons (see table 2.1, item 5); the Prelude and Fugue in A Minor, WoO posthum 9, Fugue in A♭ Minor, WoO 8 (first published in 1864 in a supplement to the *Allgemeine musikalische Zeitung*), and *Geistliches Lied*, op. 30 (see table 2.1, item 10); and a fugal Kyrie with basso continuo, WoO 17, three movements of the so-called *Missa canonica*, WoO 18, and early versions of the first two of the *Drei geistliche Chöre*, op. 37 (see table 2.1, item 11). In the following remarks, I examine a representative sampling of this impressive body of work.[11]

11. At first Brahms kept with his original plan to preserve his exercises – "Keep all the music sheets that you have sent me," he instructed his friend in a letter of 27 April 1856. "I will do

Example 2.1: Joachim, circle canon
(transcription from *Briefwechsel*, 5:133; realization supplied).

* * *

On 25 April 1856 Brahms happily acknowledged receipt of Joachim's initial batch of studies, which had been delivered in three installments during the previous week.[12] Most of this letter was given over to discussing the declining condition of Schumann, whom Brahms had recently visited in Endenich; two days later, however, Brahms responded at length to Joachim's work. He began by making some general, discouraging remarks about his friend's fugue subjects on B–A–C–H (pl. 2.1) and then turned to a study that Joachim had inscribed "Zirkel-Kanon" (ex. 2.1): "I don't understand how the 'circle canon' in your

---

so, too; then perhaps after a long time we will look at them together and, I hope, [see] great progress" (ibid., 138). An older, more reticent Brahms later destroyed most of these pieces, however, burning them in the 1880s in an "auto-da-fé," if we are to believe Max Kalbeck (*Brahms*, 1:262–63). Among the lost works, ironically, must be counted all the pieces that were first sent to Joachim on 27 April 1856 (see table 2.1, item 5), including Brahms's own canonic imitations over the *Art of Fugue* subject as well as a four-voice circle canon and several free instrumental canons (about which Joachim wrote admiringly [*Briefwechsel*, 5:142]). Still, a good number of studies survived in completed compositions – some, as we have seen, in works that Brahms himself eventually published; others, including the Prelude and Fugue in A Minor and the Mass movements, in autographs or copies kept by friends. Joachim, by contrast, did hold on to his studies, most of which are preserved in the Joachim Nachlaß.

12. *Briefwechsel*, 5:133–36.

Plate 2.1. Joseph Joachim, fugal studies on B–A–C–H, autograph. Hamburg, Staats- und Universitätsbibliothek Carl von Ossietzky, Nachlaß J. Joachim, Sign. 83; reprinted with permission.

Plate 2.2. Joseph Joachim and Johannes Brahms, miscellaneous contrapuntal studies, autograph. Hamburg, Staats- und Universitätsbibliothek
Carl von Ossietzky, Nachlaß J. Joachim, Sign. 1974.6; reprinted with
permission.

{41}

Example 2.2: Brahms, circle canon after a subject of Joachim's
(cf. plate 2.2).

last letter comes by its name. It ends reasonably in A major and can, of course, also be played in F [*recte:* B] major. The entry [of the second voice] can occur only in the last bar, and that is not enough."[13] As Brahms had noted, the *dux* of Joachim's canon is presented entirely in the key of A major and then, by means of a new clef and key signature, is simply transposed downward a minor seventh into the key of B major. The conceit is clever, but the result is utterly impractical. Were the pattern of transposition by descending minor sevenths to be pursued, the music would soon range impossibly low. To illustrate proper technique, Brahms sent his own example, which follows the traditional scheme of the *canon per tonos* (see the piece headed "Kreis-Kanon" in pl. 2.2, transcribed in ex. 2.2). Reworking the first four measures of Joachim's subject, he wrote a new *dux* that modulates upward from A major to B major; accordingly, the little piece would come full circle after six statements with a return to the opening key.

13. Ibid., 136–37. For a brief discussion of the leaf containing the fugue subjects on B–A–C– H, see Isolde Vetter, "Johannes Brahms und Joseph Joachim in der Schule der alten Musik," in *Alte Musik als ästhetische Gegenwart: Bach, Händel, Schütz: Bericht über den internationalen musikwissenschaftlichen Kongreß Stuttgart 1985*, ed. Dietrich Berke and Dorothee Hanemann, 2 vols. (Kassel: Bärenreiter, 1987), 1:461–62. The first subject is inscribed "*schlecht.* Besessenes hin u. hertaumeln" (*bad.* Madman staggering back and forth); the second, "besser, zu unentschieden" (better, too undecided). The autograph of Joachim's "circle canon" is lost, but a transcription appears in *Briefwechsel,* 5:133.

Example 2.3: Joachim, canon study on F–A–E (cf. plate 2.2).

Next Brahms took up Joachim's two-voice inversion canon (see the first piece in pl. 2.2, transcribed in ex. 2.3). The *dux* of this unusual study begins with the notes of the violinist's personal motto, F–A–E (meaning *Frei aber einsam*); the resolution – left for Brahms to solve and written in his own hand – sets out with notes spelling the name of Joachim's erstwhile fiancée, Gisela von Arnim (Gis–E–La), whose termination of the engagement some years earlier had given Joachim both his *Freiheit* and his *Einsamkeit*.[14] The conception, again, was clever, but the counterpoint had its infelicities. The piece seemed "empty in places," Brahms wrote, referring to several of the octaves that he had duly marked in the score. Although he saw no fault in those occurring in mm. 6 and 5a (both are approached by step in contrary motion and involve a doubling of the implied chord root E), he took exception to those in m. 4 (probably because of the overly wide registral disjunction between the voices) and in mm. 3 and 8 (no doubt because of the awkward treatment there of the surrounding dissonance).[15] By contrast, the F-major canon appearing on the same bifolio, whose final measure Brahms marked "Schön," almost escapes censure; his only suggestion regarding this little piece was to change the B♭ in m. 6 of the *comes* (and presumably also that on the downbeat of the following measure) to B♮, thereby forming a smooth vii$^6_5$/V passing chord rather than the unusual harmony of IV$^6_5$ (see pl. 2.2).

Although Joachim gratefully received Brahms's "lesson on the circle canon," as he put it in a letter of 4 May, and complimented the origi-

---

14. Joachim mentioned the counterpoint exchange to Gisela von Arnim for the first time in a letter written ca. 26 April 1856 (see *Joachim Briefe*, 1:339). In a postscript to his letter of 25 April, Brahms indicated that he had been quick to solve this canon: "In the canon f–a–e is easily solved by g♯–e–a" (*Briefwechsel*, 5:136). Joachim had explained the significance of an earlier association of these motives in a letter of 29 November 1853, when, in response to the congratulations that Schumann had conveyed upon hearing that the couple were planning to be married, he sent his *Drei Stücke für Violine und Pianoforte*, op. 5: "The second piece, which should really be inscribed Malinconia, contains the answer to the question of the bridegroom business; the final notes accentuated with blue ink F–A–E, which alternate in the course of the piece with three other notes [G♯–E–A], have not merely an artistic but a general human significance for me: their meaning is 'frei aber einsam.' I am not engaged" (*Joachim Briefe*, 1:109). A slightly different reading of this letter, together with excerpts from the piece in question, is given in Andreas Moser, *Joseph Joachim: Ein Lebensbild*, rev. and enlarged ed., 2 vols. (Berlin, 1908), 1:189–90. See also the references to Joachim's correspondence with Frl. von Arnim in Hans Kohlhase, "Brahms und Mendelssohn: Strukturelle Parallelen in der Kammermusik für Streicher," in *Brahms und seine Zeit*, 65. As Brahms would have noted, the "Fugenthema" found on this leaf begins with an embellished retrograde of Joachim's motto – and one sanctioned by Schumann, who on the title page of the well-known collaborative "F–A–E Sonata" wrote "**F.A.E.** In Erwartung der Ankunft des verehrten und geliebten Freundes Joseph Joachim schrieben diese Sonate: Robert Schumann, Albert Dietrich und Johannes Brahms" (In anticipation of the arrival of the admired and beloved friend Joseph Joachim, this sonata was written by Robert Schumann, Albert Dietrich, and Johannes Brahms).

15. In order to avoid similar empty octaves in his "Kreis-Kanon," Brahms altered the head of the subject after its initial appearance (compare in ex. 2.2 the second half of the second beat of m. 1 with the analogous parts of mm. 5 and 9).

nality in voice leading and the "rich and smooth" harmony of Brahms's own specimen,[16] he does not seem to have acted on his friend's advice regarding the other two pieces. The offending octaves, at all events, re-appeared in a three-voice fugue that was probably based on the "good, short" fugue subject that he mentioned in the same letter and whose final exposition is derived from the F–A–E canon. By the same token, in his later revision for organ of the F-major canon, Joachim retained the diatonic reading of the chord that Brahms had questioned.[17]

Examination of one last study by Joachim will serve to illustrate his bemused attitude toward the whole enterprise. To be sure, the com-poser promised Brahms that the music he was sending under his cover letter of 30 April, consisting of several canons and one variation on the Irish *Elfenlied*, would be "more humane" than his earlier offerings (see table 2.1, item 6); yet included in this package was a seven-voice piece that is at once bizarre and humorous (bottom of plate 2.3 and ex. 2.4).[18] The bass – which, tellingly, unites the Gisela and Joachim mottos in a kind of musical marriage – is imitated in retrograde motion by the tenor,

16. *Briefwechsel*, 5:140.

17. Joachim apparently never sent either piece for Brahms's examination. The fugue is preserved in Joachim Nachlaß, Sign. 61. For a facsimile of a part of the autograph of the canon for organ (Joachim Nachlaß, Sign. 64), see Vetter, "Brahms und Joachim in der Schule der alten Musik," 470. Vetter mistakenly identifies this version as the F-major canon to which Brahms was responding in his letter of 27 April 1856 (ibid., 462–63). Joachim clearly was fond of the little canon; he set down yet another version in what seems to have been an entry in an autograph book (reproduced in J. A. Fuller-Maitland, *Joseph Joachim* [London: J. Lane, 1905], facing p. 56).

18. *Briefwechsel*, 5:138. With the exception of one *Elfenlied* variation, these studies are pre-served on a mutilated bifolio in the composer's estate (Joachim Nachlaß, Sign. 58); the missing variation probably had been written on the bottom half of fol. 2r, which was later cut off from the rest, perhaps when, during the summer, Joachim returned to the *Elfenlied* to write a longer series of variations (see table 2.1, items 10 and 12). Joachim's treatment of the tune is discussed in Michael Struck, "Dialog über die Variation – präziert: Joseph Joachims 'Variationen über ein irisches Elfenlied' und Johannes Brahms' Variationenpaar op. 21 im Licht der gemeinsamen gattungstheoretischen Diskussion," in *Musikkulturgeschichte: Fest-schrift für Constantin Floros zum 60. Geburtstag*, ed. Peter Petersen (Wiesbaden: Breitkopf & Härtel, 1990), 105–54. Struck's dating of Joachim's first canons and initial variation using the Irish tune as from the "beginning of June" (ibid., 108) is erroneous. It is, rather, the more ambitious variation set that was composed in June (and revised, in accordance with Brahms's suggestions, in July); this is preserved in a separate manuscript (Joachim Nachlaß, Sign. 59) and has recently been edited by Struck (*Variationen über ein irisches Elfenlied für Klavier* [Ham-burg, J. Schuberth, 1989]).

Plate 2.3. Joseph Joachim, canon studies, autograph. Hamburg, Staats-
und Universitätsbibliothek Carl von Ossietzky, Nachlaß J. Joachim, Sign.
58; reprinted with permission.

Example 2.4: Joachim, canon study, "Schulfuchserei" (cf. plate 2.3).

an idea that is realized, too, in the composer's playful treatment of the text "Schulfuchserei!" (Pedantry), which the tenor gives as "Ei! Er Schulfuchs!" (which might be translated as "Alas! Pedant!"). Resting on this framework is a second, five-part canon (bringing to mind nothing so much as Webern's Concerto, op. 24). The two halves of the *dux*, given out in a series of fourteen quarter notes, are treated separately by the remaining four voices, which, as partially indicated by Joachim's ceremonious inscriptions, imitate the material in prime, inversion, and retrograde inversion forms and in diminution and double diminution.[19]

Joachim was no faster in responding to Brahms's initial studies than he had been in making his own. After holding on to his partner's first canons for nearly a month, he returned them without comment on 22 April 1856; and even though Brahms had sent them back for review in

19. Brahms's own bemusement can be noted in his remark that "the pedant [*Schulfuchs*] . . . seems more serious than it is" (*Briefwechsel*, 5:143).

his letter of 27 April – together with a batch of instrumental exercises – Joachim, who was making ready for a journey to Vienna and Italy, left his friend awaiting a response until 1 June, when he arrived in Heidelberg on his return journey. This belated evaluation took a more "poetic" than "technical" tone:

> Some distractions by me, which I have written in pencil, have stolen into your last works, also the first vocal canons. I especially love the Benedictus because of its pure harmony – the steel-like harshnesses, which have a somewhat noble solemnity, don't disturb me. In the case of the five-voice canon in augmentation, I like the courageous hoping spirit – I think God must love us if we can pray in this manner! The answer [to the prayer] is already contained somewhat in the song – I don't feel so guiltless and probably would have prayed more humbly. The Lord bless you! The wide disposition of the harmonies with the bold independence of the individual voices I will gladly excuse, but [I] would like to hear it in order to be completely reassured.
>
> About the other free canons for instruments I can speak only admiringly. How far ahead of me are you [in these matters]! Yet I cannot deny that the first entries of the deeply felt circle canon seem contrapuntally harsh, empty. Of course, if an Aeolian harp played it, or if we had string instruments with pedals, thereby sustaining the harmony, then it would have been magnificent.[20]

---

20. Ibid., 141–42. Although the letter is headed "Heidelberg am 1ten Mai," it is clear from the context that it was written on 1 June, as noted by the editor of the correspondence, Andreas Moser. Joachim apparently included a hasty note that he had written the previous day but had been unable to post: "From Heidelberg, where I am arriving just before the post office closes, I send you your compositions; for the last time without my own. . . . Tomorrow I will write more; today I only wanted to take advantage of the [longer opening time of] Saturday to send you your things" (ibid., 141). The first paragraph of Sunday's letter not only clarifies the matter of dating but, more important, suggests that Joachim might now have included some new studies of his own: "Yesterday, when I wanted [to go] to the post office to dispatch your parcel, it had gotten too late; the people here closed it already at seven instead of eight. Now today comes a bulkier but more aesthetic double fine [*ein voluminöser, aber ästhetischer Straf-Doppeltaler*]! True Heidelberg wares, which you will welcome!" (ibid.). The penalty, in other words, would seem to have been paid in new studies ("true Heidelberg wares"). Although we can only speculate regarding the identity of this music, an autograph containing eight two-part canons at various intervals (all but one of which is set over a free voice), preserved in Hanover, Staatsbibliothek, offers itself as a likely candidate. Significantly, these pieces bring to mind the set of canonic imitations on the *Art of Fugue* subject, which Joachim was then working to complete. I wish to thank Professor Christopher Reynolds for drawing my attention to these exercises.

Of this collection only the two vocal canons have survived. The Bene-dictus is surely the canonic setting that Brahms had reported making on 25 February 1856 to Clara Schumann (and that was soon to form a part of the *Missa canonica* and later to turn up in the motet "Warum," op. 74, no. 1).[21] We can be nearly as certain that the five-voice augmentation canon was the first version of the canon of that type in the later motet "Schaffe in mir, O Gott," op. 29, no. 2. In his evaluation, Joachim implied that the text of this canon was a prayer, and so, too, is that in op. 29, which begins with the petition "Create in me a clean heart, O God, and renew a right spirit within me." Moreover, when, in September 1860, Brahms sent both of the recently completed op. 29 motets to Joachim, he described them as "partly known," to which Joachim re-sponded, "In part of the vocal pieces I have again greeted a dear old friend."[22]

That Brahms's initial pair of studies eventually saw print is not surpris-ing; the composer's high intentions had been expressed clearly in his own commentary on them: "Not taking into account the artifice, is it good music? Do the artifices make it more beautiful and valuable?"[23]

---

21. See Brahms's letter to Clara of 26 February 1856: "Yesterday I wrote a little Benedictus (canonic) for four voices" (*Schumann-Brahms Briefe*, 1:178).

22. *Briefwechsel*, 5:288, 290. In the preface to his recent first edition of Brahms's collected Mass movements, based on recently recovered copies in the hand of Brahms's friend Julius Otto Grimm, Otto Biba misinterprets Joachim's remarks in his letter of 1 June 1856 (not 1 May, as cited there) and in so doing mistakenly identifies the five-voice augmentation canon in question as the original version of the four-voice Benedictus (see Johannes Brahms, *Messe*, ed. Otto Biba [Vienna: Doblinger, 1984], [iii]–[iv]). On 10 September 1857, Grimm asked the composer for the favor of sending him "the leaf on which your canon from Psalm 51 'Schaffe mir Gott ein rein Herz' is written as a *Dublette*" (*Briefwechsel*, 4:57). Margit McCorkle has suggested that Grimm was requesting here a draft of the *third* section of op. 29, no. 2 ("Tröste mich wieder mit deiner Hilfe"), evidently understanding "Dublette" to refer to the bipartite construction of that canon, which is introduced by the tenors and basses and then echoed by the sopranos and altos (McCorkle, 98). That interpretation seems doubtful to me, however. It is much more likely that Grimm used the word, not in any technical sense, but to mean what Brahms had meant by it in his letter to Clara Schumann of 30 November 1855, where he described his joy at being permitted to take duplicate copies of music (*Doubletten*) from the collection of his Hamburg friend Theodor Avé-Lallement (see n. 8 above). Thus Grimm's remark – which quotes the text of the opening section of the motet, after all, not the third – may be understood as a request for a duplicate copy of the augmentation canon that Brahms had composed during the previous year. There is no evidence, finally, that any other part of the motet was written before 1860.

23. *Briefwechsel*, 5:138.

And his successful integration of "artifice" and "good music" is demonstrated not only in the early Benedictus and augmentation canon but in three longer works dating from April – the Prelude and Fugue in A Minor for organ; the *Geistliches Lied*, a beautiful double canon at the ninth for chorus and organ accompaniment; and the Organ Fugue in A♭ Minor, whose obsessive deployment of the opening subject (here in inversion, diminution, and augmentation, there in stretto and syncopation) only enhances the deep expression of this extraordinary work.[24]

Brahms mailed this collection on 5 June, having at last received word from Joachim in Heidelberg:

> I would have sent the two fugues long ago but had no address. How do you like them? Write me at length about them, as much, whether bad or good, as you find to say? I have of course been practicing the organ lately, from which these [pieces] come. No doubt the canon [op. 30] does not especially please you? The interludes are quite terrible? The Amen (I mean the word generally) will do; that part pleases me the most. . . . What do you think of the beginning of the A♭-Minor Fugue? It gives me pangs of conscience. A♭ minor is clearly established through the prelude. I consider the answer to be at the fifth.[25]

Perhaps driven by his own guilty conscience, Joachim quickly responded, and in a letter of ca. 16 June 1856, in which he posted his first new work in some six weeks, he sent thoughtful commentary on each of the three pieces.[26]

First to be considered was the Prelude and Fugue in A Minor, which was delightful "on account of its bold, fast-moving life." Joachim questioned whether the syncopated passage occurring in mm. 10–12 was

24. In his own handwritten catalog of published works, Brahms assigned the date of April 1856 to both the A♭-Minor Fugue and the *Geistliches Lied* (Orel, 534). The Prelude and Fugue in A Minor, which was not published until 1927, is not listed in Brahms's catalog, of course; but, as we shall discover, it must have been composed at around the same time as the other pieces. Furthermore, from Brahms's failure to dispatch any of these works to Joachim in his package of 27 April, we may deduce that none was yet finished at that time. The whole impressive set, therefore, must have been completed at around the turn of the month.

25. *Briefwechsel*, 5:142–44. There is no evidence that Brahms ever composed a prelude for this fugue.

26. Ibid., 144–49. This lengthy letter, from which the next several quotations are drawn, is headed "Heidelberg, Juni" but may be more closely dated on the basis of Joachim's remark therein that he was late by one day in corresponding because he had received Brahms's latest shipment only eight days earlier.

properly suited to the organ. Although in this case he was quick to allow
that Brahms probably knew best – he addressed his friend here as "ve-
rehrter Herr Dom-Organist *in spe*" – he expressed his objection to the
"harsh" passage in mm. 14–15 in no uncertain terms. The "displaced
suspensions I understand, to be sure – but – beautiful it's not. Maybe
something else will occur to you, original and beautiful. Especially with
the first C♯/D♯ [last beat of m. 14] one is not sufficiently prepared for
the C♯. . . . It made me quite sad each time I, otherwise with great
pleasure, worked my way through the piece."[27] Joachim's last objection
concerning the prelude comes at the very end, following the cadence in
the Neapolitan key of B♭ in m. 27. "It begins there to breathe so beautifully," he noted, but then "goes all at once quickly to the end, not
majestic enough for the design, it seems to me."

Turning to the fugue, Joachim opined that its "value . . . equals that of
the beautiful prelude; a rich theme and even richer working out. How
lofty the first episode and the progression to the counterexposition!
How beautiful the gentle B major! – with the proper registers it must
sound very effective. I felt myself physically transformed into a listener
in a church." Again, however, Joachim was disturbed by Brahms's rush-
ing headlong into an inportant structural moment. Evidently referring
to m. 41, he wrote that he "would have liked it if there were a bit more
improvisation in E minor (perhaps related to the figure of the first
episode, *piano*), so that the return to the main motive with the pedal
countertheme [in m. 42] might enter in all its majesty!" And again,
probably in m. 52, Joachim was troubled by a C♯, which sounded "horrible . . . every time." But a passage that he indicated by "many exclamation marks" – surely the pedal point beginning in m. 57, with its frenetic
quotation from the beginning of the prelude – virtually transported the
critic:

> That must have an Ur-Bachian-Handelian sound on the organ – and
> especially if the organist can hardly keep calm for joy and just tears loose
> at the organ, very strong, with four-foot stops, and if the pedal for his part
> cannot again hold out any longer, in the consciousness of his much more

27. As Brahms noted in his response to this letter (ibid., 149), he had inadvertently omitted a
natural sign on the last beat of m. 14. The correct reading of this passage first appeared in
George Bozarth's recent critical edition of the complete organ works (Johannes Brahms,
Werke für Orgel, ed. George S. Bozarth [Munich: G. Henle Verlag, 1987]); see also the discussion in Bozarth's "Brahms's Organ Works: A New Critical Edition," *American Organist* 22
(1988): 51.

powerful voice, but as he was made to do jumps into the middle of the measure, and in the rejoicing fingers with his proud strides, a fine old fellow who isn't bothered about the world and pushes through his own ideas of the rhythm! How I'll rejoice from the heart to hear that – dear Johannes.

The remarkable Fugue in A♭ Minor drew an even more heartfelt, if less breathless, response. "I can only express my opinion [of it]," Joachim wrote,

> by silently immersing myself in its music: I want to play it through again to myself just now, as I have already done so often. From beginning to end it is wonderfully deep; I know few pieces that have made such an impression of unity, beauty, and blissful peace on me as this fugue has. . . . [It is] a pure, genuine work of art, through and through! I'll not speak at all of the rich voice leading, and so on, all counterpoint, as significant as it is, is a matter of secondary importance here.

Secondary or not – but as "the best sign that [his] love for the piece [was] not blind" – Joachim did take note of three small contrapuntal infelicities. In the first case, involving an awkwardly harmonized "G and G♭ in the middle voice," he offered a provisional alteration, which he urged Brahms to improve; in the second, "as a pedant" he replaced the third beat of a dotted half note with a quarter-note rest ("because of the bass"). As for the third case, he expressed a hope that Brahms himself might replace some fifths with "more flawless" writing.

Joachim had still to consider the *Geistliches Lied*, which he judged "on the whole very beautiful." Yet, more emphatically than before, he encouraged Brahms to soften his pungent harmonic language:

> I have nothing at all against the Amen at the conclusion; on the contrary, I like it; the organ point must make a holy, devout effect. But there are many harsh places! For example, in the Amen in question, the tenor, which is beautiful in and of itself, clashes all too harshly with the alto and soprano at the place marked ⨍! Your ear is so used to rugged harmony in a polyphonic texture of this kind that you rarely think about the voices solely on the basis of their relation to one another – because with you what is proper in that regard is associated equally with what completes it. You can't ask for that from a listener, even the most musical one; and since in the end all art is meant to bring pleasure, since that is its most sacred privilege, I ask you to think it over. Often (in all your things) it spoils my unalloyed pleasure, which otherwise they give me as do those of no other living composer.

Example 2.5: Brahms, *Geistliches Lied*, op. 30, mm. 58–61.

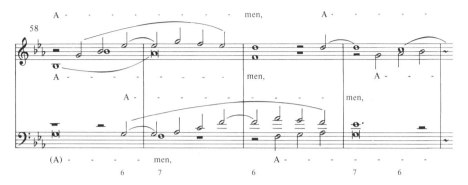

"I am quite happy you like the fugues," Brahms wrote in his apprecia-
tive response of 22 June. "You are right about all you assign, and everything will be changed when you see them again. . . . I had noticed the
fifths at the end of the A♭-Minor [Fugue] but found them acceptable at
the time. I will see."[28] In spite of this promise, Brahms does not seem to
have returned any of the pieces; nor did he preserve any of the manuscripts on which Joachim had entered his annotations. The only extant
autograph of the A-Minor Fugue, to be discussed more fully below, is
one that Brahms had given Clara Schumann in early May and so is
untouched by any revision inspired by his friend's criticism. In the case
of the *Geistliches Lied*, Brahms seems simply to have ignored Joachim's
advice; at any rate, the succession of harsh harmonies occurring in the
"Amen" just after the entrance of the majestically soaring tenor melody
(m. 59 in the published version) is very likely the uncompromising
passage that his friend had censured (ex. 2.5). There the tenor, which
had entered in unison with the bass on the final beat of the previous
measure, lingers on its initial G before making its flight and thereby
briefly sounds an expressive major second against the bass (and minor
ninth against the alto). Meanwhile, the soprano, whose E♭ initiates an
artful chain of 7–6 suspensions, only intensifies the harmony, as it leaps
to a dissonant G on the second beat, from which peak the line finally
heads toward a belated resolution of the seventh in m. 60.

With the A♭-Minor Fugue, however, matters are somewhat different.
As Susan Testa has shown, changes made in m. 39 of the sole surviving
autograph of this work (held in a private American collection) – which
Brahms sent to Clara Schumann in early June, recovered later in the

28. *Briefwechsel*, 5:149–50.

summer (after he had read Joachim's comments), and then belatedly returned in 1864 (just after the fugue had been published) – surely were stimulated by Joachim's first objection; here, through a simple rhythmic realignment, the composer brought about certain improvements in the offending harmonies surrounding the G and G♭ in the middle voice.[29] Perhaps this realignment merely reflected Joachim's own provisional reading; at all events, Brahms still was not satisfied, and in the text used in the first edition he refined the passage further, above all through changes in register. The first edition, moreover, shows signs of a reaction to Joachim's second critical comment; there, in m. 54, Brahms replaced the dotted half note B♭ occurring in the corresponding passage of the autograph (m. 43) with a half note and a quarter-note rest. In the end, only the fifths appearing at the conclusion of the fugue (mm. 45–46 of the autograph; mm. 56–57 of the first edition) remained unaffected by Joachim's commentary.[30]

* * *

In his next studies, Brahms turned from the high Baroque keyboard style in which the organ fugues are rooted to vocal models drawn from the more distant past. Dating from June are a fugal Kyrie in G Minor for four-voice choir and basso continuo and a number of canonic settings of Latin texts. When submitting this hefty collection to Joachim on 22 June, Brahms was characteristically self-effacing:

> I am hardly working; nothing other or more than you see. . . . The Kyrie I am sending is merely a study. The other pieces belong to a (forthcoming) Mass in C Major for five voices. The Agnus Dei follows after the F-major Benedictus, which you know. Before the Sanctus is the Amen of the Credo,

29. Susan Testa, "A Holograph of Johannes Brahms's Fugue in A-Flat Minor for Organ," *Current Musicology* 19 (1975): 89–102. This article includes a facsimile of the autograph, the first edition of which appears as Anhang A in Bozarth's recent critical edition (see n. 27 above).

30. As Virginia Hancock has observed (*Brahms's Library of Early Music*, 77), in his copy of *Der vollkommene Capellmeister*, Brahms took note of Mattheson's nondogmatic remarks concerning the avoidance of consecutive fifths, as expressed in passages such as "I wish in no way to defend careless fifthmakers, and I have the appropriate aversion for such impure phrases. . . . Yet one must also judge the thing sensibly, and must not straight away pour out the baby with the bath water" (Ernest C. Harriss, *Johann Mattheson's "Der vollkommene Capellmeister": A Revised Translation with Critical Commentary* [Ann Arbor, Mich.: UMI Research Press, 1981], 514).

in C major. Perhaps I'll enclose another two innocent canon melodies. . . .
Is there not too much modulating in a Mass if the Sanctus and Hosanna
are in A♭, the Benedictus is in F, the Agnus goes from F minor to A minor,
and the whole Mass in C major?[31]

These pieces, so unceremoniously introduced, made a deep impression on Joachim. "Your works have astonished me," he wrote in mid-
July; "they are so artful, deeply felt. I want to study them even more
closely in order to give better reasons for my views than if I return them
today."[32] Joachim was good to his word and within a short time had
sent some thoughtful commentary. He began with the Kyrie, which he
judged "in spirit certainly more than a 'study.' " Such a description, he
continued, was

> applicable only to the carelessly large range that you give the parts, not to
> the value of the character, which has about it nothing dry or predictable.
> The theme is lovely to me, and the counterexposition beautiful; also the
> countertheme. I especially like the beginning of the middle section, and
> then especially where it appears in the tenor, united with the main idea.
> That seemed significant to you, too! The first organ point on the sub-
> dominant sounds noble, and the last, with the rich counterpoint, signifi-
> cant: in short, the whole piece is full of beauty and deserves to be used by
> you. Perhaps you might broaden things here and there; often it seems to
> me too tight, crowded; here and there one would like some peaceful
> measures. It would be good to make the entrances even more promi-
> nent.[33]

The composer betrays his stylistic orientation at the outset of the
piece, which virtually quotes Mattheson's example, in *Der vollkommene
Capellmeister*, of *contrapunto doppio alla Zoppa*, involving "a counterpoint
whose notes are so syncopated against the regular meter that they so to

---

31. *Briefwechsel,* 5:151. Brahms actually reveals an "organic" approach to tonal relations
among the various sections. Although, as he noted, the Sanctus is in A♭, it begins in octaves on
the note C and thus follows smoothly from the preceding Credo (which, Brahms tells us, was
to be in C major). At the same time, the Hosanna leads felicitously to the following movement. It begins in A♭, to be sure; but by ending with a half cadence in F minor it prepares the
key in which the Agnus Dei begins.

32. Ibid., 155. In the third edition of the published correspondence, this letter is entered as
no. 109 and given a suggested date of "Anf[ang] Juli 1856." It is clear from the context that it
stems from the middle of the month and that it was written a day or so *before* the letter that was
published as no. 108 (and given the suggested date of "Juni 1856").

33. Ibid., 152.

Example 2.6: *a*, After Mattheson, *Der vollkommene Capellmeister.*
b, Brahms, Kyrie, WoO 17, mm. 1–6.

speak limp or stumble: as is considered very artistic in the so-called
Allabreve style" (ex. 2.6).[34] Having so invoked the *stile antico*, Brahms
then explores all manner of contrapuntal artifice. Thus, the opening
Kyrie offers a fugal exposition, with subject, answer, and countersubject,
each appearing in both prime and inverted forms, and then quickly
gives way to a final statement of the subject in the tonic, set over a
"noble" subdominant pedal point. The Christe, remaining true to the
alla Zoppa style, offers an angular, syncopated subject – here is unfolded
the "carelessly large range" that disturbed Joachim – and is treated in a
free, imitative fashion, with "tight, crowded" entries beginning on G, A♭,
B♭, and C (ex. 2.7). The work concludes, in the impressive manner noted
by Joachim, with a lengthy passage in which the Kyrie and Christe subjects are not only combined (ex. 2.8*a*) but worked out in double counterpoint and set over the countersubject in the bass (ex. 2.8*b*).

This Kyrie was sent in a package also containing unaccompanied
canonic settings of the Sanctus, Agnus Dei, and Dona nobis pacem.[35] As

34. *Johann Mattheson's "Der vollkommene Capellmeister,"* 770.

35. After having been lost for several decades, all four movements recently came to light
again in Massachusetts, in copies made in 1857 by J. O. Grimm. In 1980, the manuscripts
were acquired at auction by the GdM and have since been published (see n. 22 above). As is
clear from Grimm's letter to Brahms of 10 September 1857, the copies were made from
manuscripts gathered in a "book" in which Brahms had preserved his contrapuntal studies
(*Briefwechsel*, 4:55–57). Evidently, Brahms had lent Grimm these manuscripts in the hopes of

Example 2.7: Brahms, Kyrie, WoO 17, mm. 27–34.

Brahms explained in his cover letter, the three *a cappella* pieces were to be joined by the earlier Benedictus as parts of a projected Mass in C; and, as we now know, in 1877, long after the idea of completing this *Missa canonica* had been abandoned, the Agnus Dei, Benedictus, and Dona nobis pacem resurfaced in the motet "Warum."[36] What evidently has gone unremarked before, however, is Brahms's fleeting (and ironic) reference in this letter to an additional pair of "innocent canonic melodies."

Here, I think, the composer alluded to early versions of "O bone Jesu" and "Adoramus te, Christe," pieces that have been fairly described as "Studienwerke" but that nonetheless eventually saw print as the open-

having his friend perform some of the works with his Göttingen choir, as is suggested by Joachim's letter to Brahms of ca. 16 March 1857: "Of your vocal pieces the Hosanna and Benedictus sound very good . . . ; the parts should go on to Göttingen" (ibid., 5:107). (In the third edition of the published correspondence, this letter is registered as no. 74 and given the erroneous date of "Ende März 1855"; the proper date can be established through a comparison of its contents with those of Joachim's letter of 18 March 1857 to Woldemar Bargiel [*Joachim Briefe*, 1:421].) By May Grimm had Brahms's "book" in hand and was able to send him a thorough (and thoroughly admiring) critique of the Mass movements, whose only fault lay in the "impossibly" low register of the alto parts (*Briefwechsel*, 4:51–52).

36. See Robert Pascall, "Brahms's *Missa canonica* and Its Recomposition in His Motet 'Warum' Op. 74 No. 1," in *Brahms 2*, 111–36.

Example 2.8: Brahms, Kyrie, WoO 17: *a*, mm. 41–46; *b*, mm. 62–67.

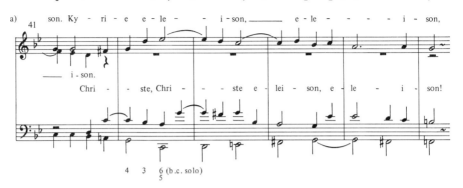

ing numbers of the *Drei geistliche Chöre*, op. 37 (1865).[37] In the engraver's model for this edition (although not the print itself), the two works in question are inscribed "(Canone) Resoluzione in 4ta, in 5ta, in 8va," and "(Canone, per arsin et thesin, et per motum contrarium)," headings that would have allowed the pieces to be resolved with only the *dux* – the "canonic melody" – given. We know, moreover, that the melodies stem from the time when Brahms, undoubtedly working from a source in the Schumann library, copied Palestrina's *Pope Marcellus Mass* and then

37. See Philipp Spitta, "Brahms," in *Zur Musik: Sechzehn Aufsätze* (1892; reprint, Hildesheim: Georg Olms, 1976), 411. Hancock has described "O bone Jesu" as "stiff and stilted" and "Adoramus te, Christe" as "noticeably lacking in stylistic unity" (*Brahms's Library of Early Music*, 110). In concluding his analysis of the latter work, Hans Michael Beuerle is more generous, arguing that it is "not the shortcoming but rather the dominance of technique [that] indicates the study-character of this composition" (*Johannes Brahms: Untersuchungen zu den A-cappella-Kompositionen, Ein Beitrag zur Geschichte der Chormusik* [Hamburg: Verlag der Musikalienhandlung Karl Dieter Wagner, 1987], 143).

composed movements for a Mass of his own.[38] Perhaps it was at this time, too, that the composer came into possession of the copy he owned containing Schumann's transcriptions from Gottlieb von Tucher's *Kirchengesänge der berühmtesten älteren italiänischen Meister* (1827); significantly, the first two works in Schumann's copy are none other than settings of an "Adoramus te, Christe" and "O bone Jesu," which are ascribed (falsely) to Palestrina.[39] With its through-imitation and stepwise melodic motion, spanning a sixth in two upward sweeps, Brahms's setting of "Adoramus te, Christe," in particular, seems indebted to the Palestrina style (ex. 2.9).[40]

Example 2.9: Brahms, "Adoramus te, Christe," op. 37, no. 2, mm. 1–6.

38. The Palestrina copy (signed and dated "Johannes Brahms Juni 1856") is preserved in the composer's estate in the same miscellany that contains the Ingegneri motets (see n. 4 above); for bibliographical details, see under the entry Anh. Va, Nr. 7, in McCorkle.

39. GdM, A295. The two works are by Rosselli and Ingegneri, respectively (see Hancock, *Brahms's Library of Early Music,* 64–65).

40. In the entry for op. 37 in his *Werkverzeichnis,* the composer dated these pieces May 1859; but that, we know, establishes only when they were completed. Brahms had a practical reason for doing so in the spring of that year, inasmuch as he was just preparing for the first rehearsal of his *Hamburger Frauenchor,* scheduled for 6 June 1859, on which, indeed, "Adoramus te, Christe" and "O bone Jesu" both appeared. In this instance, moreover, the word *completed* might be taken literally. The main body of both pieces – the canonic melody, so to speak – manifests a Renaissance style that is in keeping with Brahms's studies of 1856; by contrast, the free conclusion of each stands closer to the dramatic style of Bach, whose cantatas Brahms had been studying only more recently. The lack of stylistic unity in "Adoramus te, Christe" is especially telling of a conclusion belatedly tacked on. Here, as Virginia Hancock has noted (*Brahms's Library of Early Music,* 110–11), the Palestrina-like canon (mm. 1–23) gives way in mm. 23–26 to a fleeting (and disconcerting) recollection of Bach's cantata *Christ lag in*

In a letter from the middle of July expressing genuine astonishment at all Brahms's latest offerings, Joachim included a revised version of his own current project, rather free variations on the Irish *Elfenlied*, whose first incarnation Brahms had criticized in the letter containing his Mass movements: "Tell me again what you think, completely unadorned. . . . Anyone who feels as deeply and truly as you must also, *nolens volens*, light upon the right expression, and that goes all the more for one who loves his [contrapuntal] matters and would like to understand more and more!"[41] Brahms's response to this invitation, sent on 22 July, was thorough and judicious, and he concluded with a pointed (and characteristic) request "to see stricter works . . . the next time." For once he had nothing of his own to send; a "half-finished Credo" he wanted to allow to rest.[42]

Joachim evidently took heed of Brahms's admonition to discipline himself; not only did he put aside the variations for good, but in a letter to Gisela von Arnim of 26 July he reported that he was composing a double fugue based on a theme of Beethoven's and Bach's, adding that "such labor is hard [but] indispensable if one wants to be a decent composer."[43] But Schumann's death on 29 July disrupted work, and,

---

Todesbanden, which Brahms had conducted in Detmold in 1858; this passage, in turn, is quickly superseded by an echo of the chordal Palestrina style (mm. 27–36) to bring about the close. Clara Schumann's remarks on the two canons suggest a similar compositional history for "O bone Jesu." In a letter to Brahms of 18 September 1859 she wrote, "I . . . find the Adoramus beautifully flowing in spite of the strict style; in the second ["O bone Jesu"] I noticed at once how particularly tenderly the ending fit the words 'Dein köstlich Blut,' even before I had seen that you yourself had specially marked these words for me. If only I could hear them all!" (Litzmann, *Clara Schumann*, 3:64). Surely what Clara noticed in the ending of "O bone Jesu" – Johannes had added a German translation for her benefit – was the chiastic structure of the lines carrying the text "sanguine tuo praetiosissimo" (mm. 11–18). Here, as the text turns to the image of the Precious Blood, the closely worked canon yields to word painting of a sort that derives directly from Bach – and indeed from *Christ lag in Todesbanden*. On Brahms's acquaintance at this time with Bach's cantata and the likely use of this work as a model for parts of the *Begräbnisgesang*, op. 13 (1858), see Virginia Hancock, "Brahms and Early Music: Evidence from His Library and His Choral Compositions," in *Brahms Studies*, 30–35.

41. *Briefwechsel*, 5:154–55.

42. Ibid., 156.

43. *Joachim Briefe*, 1:356. The "Beethoven'sches und Bach'sches Thema" probably was related to the fifth of the B–A–C–H themes that Brahms had seen in April (see pl. 2.1); this subject, which is inscribed "aus dem E mol–Quart: v. Beethov.," closely resembles the passage played by the cello in mm. 63ff. of the slow movement of the second "Razumovsky" Quartet.

despite Brahms's repeated encouragement for more than a year thereafter, Joachim could muster nothing else until the summer of 1857,
when he sent two packets containing a number of fugues (see table 2.2,
items 1 and 2).[44] For his part, Brahms, on whom the project had already
begun to have the desirable effect of stimulating larger works – the two
sets of Variations, op. 21, the First Piano Concerto, the two Serenades,
and a rich variety of vocal compositions all date from the later 1850s –
contributed nothing further until September 1861, when at long last,
having suggested a renewal of the exchange that might include "Kon-
trapunktisches, Walzer, Variationen und sonst Zeug," he sent the Credo
for his canonic Mass (see table 2.2, item 3).[45] But by this date Joachim had essentially given up composition, and Brahms, who was well
launched into his "first maturity," scarcely needed further instruction.
Indeed, the making of the "Handel" Variations – with its artful canons
and intricate concluding fugue – lay just behind him, and the ability to
compose the "Haydn" Variations – with its masterly invertible counterpoint and ostinato finale – now did lie firmly within his grasp.

II

In a sense the little canonic Benedictus that Brahms had written on 25
February 1856 was the mother of the entire study, inasmuch as it seems
to have stimulated the composer, on the very next day, to press Joachim

44. See *Joachim Briefe*, 1:370; and *Briefwechsel*, 5:161, 168, 175, 182, 185–86, 189, 193.

45. *Briefwechsel*, 5:305, 307, 309, 313. Brahms had already shown this piece to Clara Schumann; see her letter to Brahms of 29 July 1861: "In this brief time I have been unable to look
through the Credo – to find my way out of such a labyrinth of canons I need a lot of time. Your
expertise in such artful, difficult things is wonderful, but I'll only appreciate them if I were to
hear them beautifully sung" (*Schumann-Brahms Briefe*, 1:372). Of this composition, which
unfortunately is now lost, we know little more than that it included some canons showing
counterpoint at the twelfth (see *Briefwechsel*, 5:307). Joachim apparently returned the manuscript to Brahms when the two met in late October 1861, thus leaving no written record of his
impressions. In later years Brahms's Mass movements seem to have circulated further among
friends; the last preserved mention of the pieces appears in a letter of December 1870, in
which Brahms requested Karl Reinthaler to return the manuscript (see ibid., 3:32). Passing
mention at least should be made here too of a slightly different "musical correspondence"
that took place in the spring of 1860, which involved studies, not in strict counterpoint, but in
chorale harmonization (see ibid., 5:266, 269, 270–73, 277). Several leaves containing Joachim's chorale settings (some of which contain annotations in Brahms's hand) are preserved
in the Joachim Nachlaß and in Lübeck, Brahms-Institut (Sammlung Hofmann). Growing out
of this study, undoubtedly, was Brahms's chorale motet "Es ist das Heil uns kommen her," op.
29, no. 1, which was completed in July 1860.

Table 2.2. Brahms-Joachim *Notenkorrespondenz*,
October 1856–October 1861

Date of Letter[a]	From	Work Submitted	Work Criticized; Other Remarks
19 Oct 56 (115)	Brahms		Expresses disappointment at having not received more counterpoint from Joachim[b]
Jan 57 (123)	Brahms		Proposes a reinstitution of the counterpoint exchange
19 Jan 57 (125)	Joachim		Agrees to Brahms's proposal and requests an "assignment"
21 Jan 57 (126)	Brahms		Suggests that Joachim would benefit from some easier exercises in counterpoint and asks him to devise his own assignment; reports that he has nothing himself to send since he has been busy with other work (i.e., with opp. 15 and 21/1–2)
16 Mar 57 (74)	Joachim		Requests that the parts for the Hosanna and Benedictus, WoO 18, be sent to Grimm in Göttingen
7 May 57 (130)	Joachim		Vows to see the "counterpoint course" through the summer
6 Jun 57 (131)	Joachim		Hints that he will soon be sending some music
16 Jun 57 (132)	Brahms		Encourages Joachim to send something
30 Jun 57 (133)	Joachim	1. Three fugues (including one in B♭ minor)	
11 Jul 57 (134)	Brahms		Comments on item 1
Jul 57 (135)	Joachim	2. Two fugues	

a. All references are to *Briefwechsel*, 5 (3d rev. ed.). Italic type indicates that the date has been supplied. The number given in parentheses is the number assigned to the letter in this edition.
b. In a letter to Joachim from the previous month, Clara Schumann had reported that Brahms was eagerly awaiting his next exercises (see *Joachim Briefe*, 1:370).

5 Dec 57 (136)	Brahms		Requests more counter-point
Sep 61 (227)	Brahms		Proposes a renewal of the exchange
Sep 61 (229)	Brahms	3. Credo for *Missa canonica* (Anh. IIa, Nr. 20); includes old Sanctus, WoO 18	
3 Oct 61 (231)	Brahms		Encourages Joachim to send something
15 Oct 61 (232)	Joachim		Promises to comment soon on the Mass

to take up at last their long-discussed plan to exchange contrapuntal exercises. But what might have stimulated Brahms to set the Benedictus text in the first place? It clearly had a significant meaning for him. In the autograph of the slow movement of the First Piano Concerto, composed in January 1857 and described by Brahms as "a gentle portrait" of Clara Schumann, the main theme is written over the words "Benedictus qui venit in nomine Domini"; and, since Brahms had sometimes addressed Robert Schumann as "Mynheer Domine," we have reason to think that the blessed one to whom he alluded was the widow who bore the late composer's name.[46] It is not difficult to believe, then, that Frau Schumann would have been in Brahms's mind as he was setting this meaningful text as a canon some ten months earlier. Indeed, he announced the little piece to her in a letter written from her boudoir, as he explained, on newly purchased yellow note paper that was adorned with a spray of roses, beneath which he inscribed "Für Clara."[47] In view of Brahms's frequent use during the 1850s of musical allusions, mottos,

46. The "gentle portrait" description comes from a letter to Clara Schumann of 30 December 1856 (*Schumann-Brahms Briefe*, 1:198); in a letter written three years earlier, Brahms had addressed Robert Schumann as "Mynheer Domine" (Kalbeck, *Brahms*, 1:139). My interpretation of the meaning of the liturgical phrase in the concerto echoes those of Robert Haven Schauffler (*The Unknown Brahms* [New York: Dodd, Mead, 1933], 438–39) and Geiringer (pp. 248–49). For a convenient survey of other interpretations, see Bozarth, "Brahms's First Piano Concerto," 211–29.

47. The relevant passage is quoted in n. 21 above.

and implied texts, we would be well advised to look for extramusical references even in the contrapuntal studies – which, after all, stand as virtually the only music that Brahms composed during the last months of his romantic passion for Clara Schumann, before the evident change in his feelings that came about in the wake of Robert Schumann's death. Now, if Brahms's fugues are not "character pieces," as his benefactor had once described those of Bach, neither can they be described as mere abstract studies in contrapuntal technique. Here, and in other works involving the organ, the young composer found a disciplined environment, one in which not only to develop his craft but to pour out his soul.

* * *

In the *Geistliches Lied*, set to a seventeenth-century text by Paul Flemming, we find a portrayal, not of Clara Schumann herself, but of a scene that she had once hopefully imagined. While walking with Johannes one evening in the summer of 1854, Clara suddenly resolved to learn to play the organ, looking ahead to a time when her husband would have recovered his health and she might please him with performances of his works for this instrument. The idea so delighted her, she recorded in her diary, that she spent a sleepless night thinking about what pieces she might perform and the means by which to lure Robert into a church, where he would be surprised to find her there playing.[48]

All these images are evident at the outset of Brahms's composition (ex. 2.10). The organ's quiet introduction not only evokes an ecclesiastical atmosphere but also, through its in medias res beginning, suggests a picture that is in keeping with Clara's hope of taking Robert unawares as he entered a church in which music was already sounding. The mood is not joyous, however. The theme of Flemming's sacred song is one of consolation rather than celebration:

Laß dich nur nichts nicht dauren	Let naught afflict thee
Mit Trauren,	with grief;
Sei stille,	be calm,
Wie Gott es fügt,	as God ordains,
So sei vergnügt	and so rejoice
Mein Wille.	my will.

48. Litzmann, *Clara Schumann*, 2:323.

Example 2.10: Brahms, *Geistliches Lied*, op. 30, mm. 1–15.

Was willst du heute sorgen	Wherefore dost thou take care
Auf morgen,	for the morrow?
Der Eine	The One God
Steht allem für,	who gives thee
Der gibt auch dir	what is thine
Das Deine.	watches over us all.
Sei nur in allem Handel	Only be in all thy doings
Ohn' Wandel,	unchanging,
Steh feste,	steadfast.
Was Gott beschleußt,	What God decrees,
Das ist und heißt	that is and shows
Das Beste.	the best.
Amen!	Amen!

But these verses are surely fitting since Schumann's condition was growing steadily worse during the spring of 1856 and a recovery looked out of the question. Brahms had discovered the awful truth at first hand when he visited Schumann in late April, at precisely the time when the work in question was composed. In this light, the *Geistliches Lied*, with its gentle *Stimmung* and encouragement to faith in adversity, might fairly be seen as a representation of how Johannes imagined conveying to Clara the sad news of Robert's horrifying decline.[49]

The other works from this time recount a different kind of autobiographical tale, one whose telling was encouraged, whether wittingly or not, by Brahms's partner in the contrapuntal exchange. Among Joachim's first studies, as we have seen, were a number of canons in which he paired his personal motto and a *soggetto cavato* representing Gisela von Arnim. "Much is implied there" was Brahms's laconic response to this motivic combination.[50] Although the topic was not discussed in their letters, Brahms must have known that Joachim, like himself, was struggling with a protracted but uncertain affair of the heart. By now Gisela was being courted by the art historian and writer Hermann Grimm (whom she eventually married). In spite of that, Joachim visited Berlin for an extended stay in the Arnim home toward the end of the summer of 1856. This event drew Clara Schumann's reproof: "You wish to steel

49. On 25 April the composer reported pessimistically to Joachim concerning his recent visit to Endenich and reminded his friend to use great discretion when speaking to Frau Schumann of her husband's condition (*Briefwechsel*, 5:134–36).

50. Ibid., 151.

your heart, to renounce a love, but you are feeding it daily. Do not exact too much from yourself, lest that novel, generous heart should succumb."[51] And whereas Grimm was no mere rival but one of Joachim's close friends – the violinist had recently written an overture to Grimm's play *Demetrius*, and the writer was Joachim's traveling companion on the journey to Vienna and Italy that he began just after having composed the very canons in question – the predicament must have seemed to Brahms all too familiar.

Brahms's own studies show a similar, if more recondite, intermingling of love and counterpoint. For his twenty-third birthday, on 7 May 1856, the composer presented Clara Schumann, who was giving concerts in London, with the Prelude and Fugue in A Minor. In lieu of a separate letter, the composer added the following lines at the end of the autograph: "So, dear Clara, while away the time on my birthday with this, then perhaps some other time. Write to me about it; is it perhaps rather stiff? Criticize it as you wish; I have another in my bag that is better. If you like it, all the better. . . . Now, a thousand greetings, take the wish for the deed. Most earnestly do I think of you now as always. Your affectionate Johannes."[52] Clara evidently responded to Johannes's invitation at once, recording in her diary that she had written to him about the piece in extenso.[53] Brahms's reply is dated 16 May: "I will not enclose my fugue again; I am practicing it just now; things are going remarkably better with the organ! By the time you return, but not a bit sooner, I will have progressed enough to play for you. Is organ playing so hard for you, too? Probably not."[54] Then, eight days later (in the first letter in which he addressed Frau Schumann with the familiar *Du*-form), he sent another copy of the fugue:

> How I would love to [join you in England]! But how could I? If [your half-brother Woldemar] Bargiel went there, people couldn't say anything, but it is just too conspicuous if I, who has no business there, come over. I have even considered that I could be a passable organ virtuoso by next year;

51. Letter of 28 September 1856, in *Joachim Briefe*, 1:370–71; English translation in *Letters from and to Joseph Joachim*, trans. Nora Bickley (London: Macmillan, 1914), 136.

52. The autograph is now in the Library of Congress, Washington, D.C. For a complete transcription of Brahms's message, see Vernon Gotwals, "Brahms and the Organ," *Music: The AGO-RCCO Magazine* 4 (April 1970): 51.

53. Litzmann, *Clara Schumann*, 2:412; Clara's letter to Johannes is lost.

54. *Schumann-Brahms Briefe*, 1:183–84.

then we could travel together, and I would shelve my piano playing for a while so that I could always tour with you. . . . I'm sending the revision of my fugue primarily because of the pretty paper (from Joachim). But it's horrible having to write so small.[55]

Brahms's sudden interest in the organ, it seems clear, must not only be understood as a logical aspect of his contrapuntal studies with Joachim but also, in view of his somewhat impulsive hope of touring together with Clara Schumann, be associated with his love for the older, married woman. Indeed, the same might be said more broadly about Brahms's determination to study counterpoint in the first place. After all, during the conversation in 1854 in which she had explained her desire to learn her husband's organ music, Clara surely would have informed Johannes of how those works had come into existence – of how nine years earlier, during one of Robert's most severe depressive episodes, she had encouraged him to join her in an intensive study of counterpoint, in the hope that the discipline required by such a project might serve to settle his mind. A pedal piano was rented, and Robert Schumann, at least, studied the organ for a time. The musical therapy was efficacious and the contrapuntal study productive: from Robert came the Studies for Pedal Piano, op. 56, Sketches for Pedal Piano, op. 58, Fugues for Organ on the Name B–A–C–H, op. 60, and Four Fugues for Piano, op. 72; from Clara, a collection of six preludes and fugues for piano, three using subjects composed by her husband (and published as op. 16) and three on subjects by J. S. Bach (which remain unpublished).[56]

Brahms must have had all this in mind when, in a passionate letter of 21 March 1855, he urged Clara to join him in his own contrapuntal project:

55. Ibid., 187–88. In his letter of 4 May Joachim had given Brahms the unusual staff paper with narrow lines so that, in the future, the manuscripts of his friend's studies might be small enough to be folded and conveniently enclosed in letters. This second copy of the Prelude and Fugue, which has not been preserved, is very likely the autograph that Brahms subsequently sent to Joachim.

56. See Peter Ostwald, *Schumann: The Inner Voices of a Musical Genius* (Boston: Northeastern University Press, 1985), 198–201; and Nancy B. Reich, *Clara Schumann: The Artist and the Woman* (Ithaca, N.Y.: Cornell University Press, 1985), 125. I am grateful to Professor Reich for information pertaining to Clara Schumann's unpublished fugues.

There was no letter from you this morning; how longingly I now await every post, every day is like an eternity to me now; I can't begin anything, can't settle myself down to work. I cannot play and even think. . . .

I'm really looking forward to one [day] when we shall pass the time, besides taking walks – with counterpoint! We should set each other exercises, the same for each, and then collect and gather them together. Should Joachim come, he must join us. We often discussed wanting to do such studies together. I think it would be wonderfully interesting and amusing, and I'll take care of [finding] some good exercises.

We must take walks very often; in the spring one cannot bear to stay inside for long.[57]

Brahms's hopes for the proposed exchange, no doubt, would have been as conflicting as his own tortured feelings were at the time – to be in close contact with Clara Schumann, to bring some order into his own unsettled life, perhaps even to effect some therapeutic benefit on Robert Schumann's behalf. We know that, upon Clara's return to Düsseldorf at the end of the month, the two did begin what she described as "theoretical studies." But these were short lived, and the most significant product of the time was something quite unlike any contrapuntal exercise: Clara Schumann's beautiful Romance in A Minor, op. 21, no. 1, presented to Brahms in an autograph that she inscribed "meinem lieben Freund Johannes componirt den 2ten April 1855" (GdM). Surely something of Clara's own confused feelings at this time is indicated by her decision, only two months later, to present her husband with the same piece, on the occasion of his forty-fifth birthday, in a copy inscribed "dem geliebten Mann am 8ten Juni 1855" (Zwickau, Robert-Schumann-Haus).

Every aspect of these earlier episodes – joint contrapuntal study, preludes and fugues, "personal works" in the key of A minor, even Clara's presentation of a "Brahms piece" on Robert's birthday – finds its echo in Brahms's organ music from 1856. Some of this can be heard in the Prelude and Fugue in A Minor that was Johannes's present for Clara on his own birthday. Not only had Clara's musical gift for him in the previous spring been written in the same key of A minor; more important, this key easily accommodates the most obvious version of what, as

57. *Schumann-Brahms Briefe*, 1:100–101.

Example 2.11: Robert Schumann, Symphony No. 4, 1st mvt.:
a, mm. 2–3; *b*, m. 29.

Brahms knew, acted in Robert Schumann's rich musico-symbolic universe as a cipher for his wife: the notes C–(L)–A–(R)–A.[58]

Schumann's Fourth Symphony – his "Clara" symphony, as he described the original version of the work, whose autograph was one of Brahms's treasured possessions – offers us the clearest model. The Clara motive, beginning on $\hat{3}$ in the key of D minor, is introduced in its "pure," scalar form at the outset of the slow introduction (ex. 2.11 *a*). But then, as the music inexorably builds toward the beginning of the frantic Allegro, an evolution takes place, leading, finally, to the main theme of the movement, which embraces the cipher in a transformation that includes an opening leap from $\hat{1}$ to $\hat{3}$ (ex. 2.11 *b*). Brahms's

58. See Eric Sams, "Did Schumann Use Ciphers," *Musical Times* 106 (1965): 584–91, esp. 584, and "Brahms and His Clara Themes," *Musical Times* 112 (1971): 432–34. There can be no question that Brahms was acquainted with Schumann's cipher. When, in a letter to Joachim from September 1854 (*Briefwechsel*, 5:59), Brahms explained that "Clara speaks" in one of the two new variations that he had recently added to the "Schumann" Variations, he was probably referring not to the first of the new variations (no. 10), in which he quotes a theme of Clara Schumann, but rather to the second (no. 11), which, as Elaine Sisman has noted, gives out the following transposed version of Schumann's theme: C–C–C–C–B–A–G♯ –G♯–A–B–C (see Elaine R. Sisman, "Brahms and the Variation Canon," *19th-Century Music* 14 [1990]: 149). Significantly, throughout this letter – and in most of Brahms's other letters to Joachim – Clara is referred to as "Frau Schumann" or (much more rarely) "Frau Clara." Only in this passage, tellingly, does Brahms write simply "Clara." For an interpretation of Brahms's First Symphony as an extended "Clara" piece, see Musgrave, 130–41; and Michael Musgrave, "Brahms's First Symphony: Thematic Coherence and Its Secret Origin," *Music Analysis* 2 (1983): 117–33. For a somewhat different account of the same subject, see my review of Musgrave, *Journal of Musicology* 7 (1989): 412–14.

Example 2.12: Brahms, Prelude and Fugue in A Minor, WoO 9: *a*, Prelude, mm. 19–20; *b*, Fugue, mm. 1–2; *c*, Fugue, mm. 42–49.

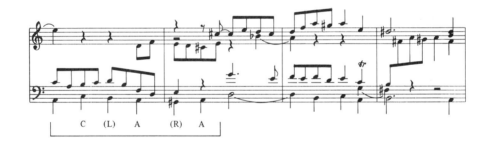

prelude and fugue shows a similar evolution, albeit one starting with the form seen in Schumann's Allegro, with its initial ascending minor third. Thus, in mm. 19–20 of the prelude, it is none other than "Clara" who is briefly suggested, but not fully embodied, in the organ pedal (ex. 2.12*a*). In this adumbrated form, she then becomes the subject of the fugue itself (ex. 2.12*b*). Finally, at the great climax of the work (mm.

42ff.), when, *sempre più forte*, the subject is given out against itself in augmentation, she twice appears, again in the pedal but now, for the first time, in her complete form, with the final note A (ex. 2.12c).[59]

This "Clara" fugue is but one side of the coin, however. On the other lies its somber companion, the Fugue in A♭ Minor, which Brahms inscribed "Ganz eigentlich für meine Clara" and presented to her in honor of Robert Schumann's birthday, on 8 June 1856.[60] Upon receiving the manuscript in London, Clara described the music as being "wunderbar schön" and, using one of Robert's most characteristic expression markings, "innig."[61] Yet Brahms's own expression marking, "Langsam (Trübe)," is more noteworthy. From Joachim, who first saw the fugue at about the same time as Frau Schumann, it elicited this response:

> The term *trübe* [gloomy, cheerless, despondent] is really not suitable – dear friend – because the mood of sadness, oppression resolves itself so gently into consolation and hope that it is at the same time uplifting. It is precisely this sinking and swelling, like breathing, that gives the piece a noble spirit that is foreign to despondency; here is life – in despondency is inactivity, stagnation. Do you know the place in Dante's *Inferno*, where monotonous sighs of the damned rise to the surface from the depths of the morass – there is nothing of this in the fugue.[62]

Had Joachim made a different literary reference – to Byron's *Manfred* or, rather, to Robert Schumann's musical treatment of the story – then he might have made more sense of Brahms's expression marking. In a breathless passage from the very letter in which he had initially proposed a counterpoint exchange, the composer thus described to Clara Schumann his feelings about this dramatic work, a gloomy tale of incestuous love that has been described as "the Romantic guilt-complex

---

59. On his birthday in 1854, Brahms had received from Julius Otto Grimm a similar present in which his own name is spelled out musically: $B(=B♭)–R–A–H(=B♮)–M–S(=E♭)$ (see Julius Otto Grimm, *Zukunfts-Brahmanen-Polka*, ed. Otto Biba [Tutzing: Hans Schneider, 1983]).

60. Compare Brahms's letter from 30 May of the following year: "I will not again send you something for June 8th, dear Clara, I would gladly have done it but I have nothing. An A♭-Minor Fugue, which one can send in the mail. . . . O, how I wished for that again!" (*Schumann-Brahms Briefe*, 1:202).

61. Litzmann, *Clara Schumann*, 2:412.

62. *Briefwechsel*, 5:147; translation after Bozarth, "Brahms's Organ Works," 52.

personified":[63] "If only I could have heard the *Manfred* music with you! That, with the *Faust*, is the most magnificent thing your husband [has] created. But I'd like to hear it as a whole and in combination with the text. What a deeply moving impression it must make. Often the melodramatic passages are incomprehensible to me, such as Astarte's appearance and speaking. That is the very highest form of musical delivery; that penetrates right into the depths of the heart."[64]

In view of the powerful impression that Schumann's work had made on Brahms, and assuming what must have been a considerable guilt complex of his own, it would not be surprising to find allusions to *Manfred* in Brahms's music from the time, least of all in a highly chromatic work conceived together with the "Clara" fugue in A minor. But if the one piece offers a fairly transparent and neutral evocation of Brahms's beloved, the other is in this sense more complex and charged. In it, I believe, Johannes sought nothing less than to identify himself with the role of Clara's spouse.

The first clues come at the outset. Remarkably enough, we have it on the composer's word, humorously expressed in July 1856 to Adolf Schubring – an early admirer who had previously written to Brahms at length about his printed compositions and had evidently now asked to see unpublished works – that he had encoded his own name in the score:

> Honestly ashamed and repenting of my negligence, yes, my misconduct, I send herewith the required replies to your kind second letter. The music is one of the replies and at the same time my autograph, for in no way do I want to attach my signature properly to it. You will probably discover the name in it and will proceed according to your letter, namely: to return it to me with vigorous reviews; I must request, however, at the first possible moment, as I have no copy of the fugues and must practice them. . . .
>
> In spite of all that, I look forward with pleasure to your appraisal of the two fugues.
>
> But there is one thing I must ask of you once and for all, namely, that you will in no way keep anything of the manuscripts, for they are unfinished and require correction, and also that you will not let them out of your house.

63. Sams, "Brahms and His Clara Themes," 434.

64. *Schumann-Brahms Briefe*, 1:100.

I greet you warmly and ask you to remain good to me. Your sincerely penitent one.[65]

The only passage in the two fugues that might conceivably represent a *soggetto cavato* of Brahms's name comes at the very beginning of the A♭-minor fugue subject (ex. 2.13*a*). Yet, significantly, this passage also offers an artful combination of two passages from Schumann's *Manfred* Overture: the pitches of the chromatic slow introduction and the rhythm and contour of the passionate second theme (ex. 2.13*b–c*). We have grounds to believe, then, that, when Brahms confessed to Joachim that this subject had caused him to develop a "guilty conscience" (*Gewissensbisse*),[66] he had in mind more than simply its tonal ambiguity. To be sure, the characteristic motive that initiates the subject is heard more easily in E♭ minor (sounding as $\hat{6}–\hat{5}–\hat{1}$) than in A♭ minor, a circumstance pertaining also to the F♮ appearing in the second measure (see ex. 2.13*a*). But this all derives from Schumann: notwithstanding its misleading signature of three flats, the *Manfred* Overture unfolds in the key of E♭ minor, and it includes a second theme that begins on the scale degrees $\hat{6}$, $\hat{5}$, and $\hat{2}$ (see ex. 2.13*c*). Moreover, with each appearance of Brahms's distinctive, laden fugue subject in its original form (e.g., mm. 5, 16, 29), the tonic key of the *Manfred* lurks underneath. The resulting ambiguity between "Schumann's key" (E♭ minor) and "Brahms's key" (the even darker A♭ minor) thus offers a suggestive metaphor for the ambiguous role that Brahms was playing in his outer life.[67]

---

65. *Briefwechsel*, 8:187–89. My translation is adapted from Styra Avins, *Letters from the Life of Johannes Brahms* (Oxford: Oxford University Press, in preparation). The "second reply" given in this letter had to do with the matter of the recent baptism of Schubring's son, for whom Brahms had acted as godfather: "I, the unnamed being, was born on the 7th of May in Hamburg, sired 9 months or so earlier by a musician of the same place. This man and his wife, my much-loved mother, are splendid people, whose copious love I can never repay. Thereupon I was baptized, learned by heart the catechism according to Luther, also read the Bible diligently, and have thereby become worthy of being listed in the Dessau church records as godfather of little Schubring. . . . Do commend me to your wife, and to little Johannes give a hearty kiss. I look forward to the time when he can study Marpurg and Mattheson with me" (Ibid., 188).

66. Ibid., 5:144.

67. The relationship between Brahms's name and the beginning of the fugue subject was first noted, without reference to Brahms's own hint, in Robert Haven Schauffler, *Florestan: The Life and Work of Robert Schumann* (1945; reprint, New York: Dover, 1963), 291n. For a largely unconvincing argument that the fugue offers instead a number of variations on the notes

Example 2.13: *a*, Brahms, Fugue in A♭ Minor, WoO 8 (original version),
mm. 1–3; *b*, Robert Schumann, *Manfred* Overture, mm. 3–6;
c, Schumann, *Manfred* Overture, mm. 217–22.

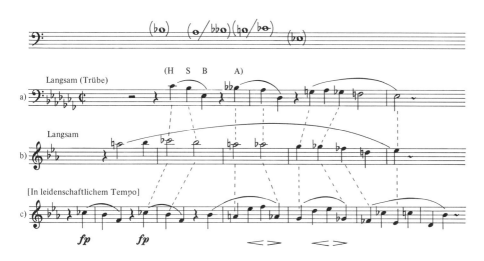

How much of this Clara Schumann sensed, we cannot know. But her
response to a letter in which Joachim had shared his impressions of
Brahms's recent works is tantalizing: "I had already written to Brahms
from London about his fugues – and think of my surprise, rather like
what you later [wrote], though, to be sure, not expressed as beautifully
and purely! The A♭-Minor Fugue in particular impressed me deeply,
what sounds, what a noble mood it has, what beautiful, devout meaning – the sixth chord toward the end, isn't it as though a holy appearance holds forth on the whole thing?"[68] This closing remark concerns the first-inversion E♭-minor harmony occurring in m. 41 (ex.
2.14), and it directs our attention again to the *Manfred* Overture. The
preceding stretto, combining an augmented, inverted form of the subject in the pedal with a detached, syncopated variation in the manual,
culminates in a chord progression that seems finally to clarify E♭ as the
dominant (II$^{6♮}_{4~3}$–V^7). Immediately, however, that sense is undermined
by the striking sonority that drew Clara Schumann's attention. Poised in
its subtly unbalanced state, this E♭-minor triad brings about a temporary
cessation of all motion. Yet harmonic equilibrium and rhythmic activity

---

B–A–C–H, see Günter Hartmann, "Zur Orgelfuge in as-Moll von Johannes Brahms," in
Brahms-Studien, vol. 7 (Hamburg: Karl Dieter Wagner, 1987), 9–19.

68. Letter of 21 July 1856, in *Joachim Briefe*, 1:356.

Example 2.14: Brahms, Fugue in A♭ Minor, WoO 8 (original version),
mm. 37 to end. Reproduced from Johannes Brahms,
Werke für Orgel, with permission of G. Henle Verlag, Munich.

are at once restored, if only briefly, by the last appearance of the fugue subject, which includes for the first time the note F♭ (m. 43), the only chromatic note from the Schumann source that Brahms had not previously used (see exx. 2.13*b* and 2.14 and cf. ex. 2.13*a*). In m. 42, the pedal supplies the root of the hovering chord and with that ultimately fixes the *soggetto cavato* within the tonic of Schumann's overture.

The autobiographical resonances in the organ pieces of April 1856 bring us, finally, to a work that we have not yet considered, the original version of the Chorale Prelude on "O Traurigkeit, o Herzeleid," WoO 7. The documentary evidence pertaining to the genesis of this music is slight. In 1882 Brahms published a revised version of the prelude, together with a fugue based loosely on the same chorale tune, in *Musi-kalisches Wochenblatt*. It is not likely, however, that the two parts were conceived together. The earliest known sources for the prelude are a copy made by Clara Schumann for her friend Carl Bogler in June 1858 (Stockholm, Stiftelsen Musikkulturens Främjande) and an autograph, now missing, that Brahms gave to his piano student Friedchen Wagner in the following month; for the fugue, an autograph presented to Philipp Spitta in the summer of 1873. Kalbeck held that the "Herzeleid" fugue was a "twin-sister" of the Fugue in A♭ Minor – a companion product of Brahms's fugal studies of 1856 – noting that in both works the subject is answered in inversion, and suggesting that in each "the composer spreads out the freshly acquired riches of his art like a many-colored carpet whose tangled ornamentation of leaf and flower sprang from one stem."[69] Reasons abound, however, to doubt this view, not the least being the lack of any mention of the fugue in the Brahms-Joachim correspondence of the time. On the other hand, we do have good grounds for assuming that the *prelude* was written during that crucial period – not, to be sure, as a part of the *Notenkorrespondenz*, but in heartfelt response to the death of Robert Schumann.[70]

In this view, Brahms's choice of the Passion chorale is readily understood: "O sorrow, o grief! is it not to be lamented? The only Child of God is borne to His grave." The form of this short "melody chorale" is no less straightforward, at least at first: the four phrases of the tune are

---

69. Kalbeck, *Brahms*, 1:266.

70. Recently, Malcolm MacDonald has suggested – erroneously, I think – that both prelude and fugue stem from the time just after Schumann's death (see his *Brahms* [New York: Schirmer, 1990], 93).

given out simply in the right hand, without ornamentation or lengthy interludes, and set over a gentle counterpoint in triplets and a firm harmonic bass (ex. 2.15*a*). The coda, however, breaks with tradition (ex. 2.15*b*). The final phrase of the chorale melody culminates, not in the expected perfect cadence, but deceptively, on a long-held vii$^6_5$/V. Then, unexpectedly, follows a return of the chorale's first phrase, transposed upward by a fourth to begin on the note A, only to be succeeded, not by a continuation of the tune but by an ornamented stepwise descent from E to A. Here, in these expressive final measures, Brahms seems to turn his attention away from the deceased composer and toward the mourning widow. Indeed, the recollected opening phrase – with its implied text "O Traurigkeit" – leads to Brahms's most moving evocation of Clara Schumann, as her motive, each note now embracing a languishing melisma, sounds forth once more.

It seems plausible, then, that the chorale prelude, like the earlier Fugue in A♭ Minor, had been written "ganz eigentlich für Clara." That assumption, in turn, raises a suggestive explanation for why the composer would have bristled when, in late June 1858, Frau Schumann reported that she had copied the music for Bogler, only to comply with Friedchen Wagner's request a few weeks later for "a souvenir" by surreptitiously hiding the piece away in her piano.[71] Perhaps there was more to Johannes's quarrel with Clara than he had allowed in his curt response of 25 June, in which he confessed his fear that she tended to praise him too highly to others; he might well have taken some added offense at an act, however well intentioned, that seemed to violate a most intimate and private musical offering. If so, then Brahms's own act of copying the music as a keepsake for Friedchen Wagner was an ironic, bittersweet gesture indeed.

* * *

Taken together, the four organ works that we have considered here unfold a touching story. The *Geistliches Lied*, in whose text we can imagine Brahms seeking the sentiments by which to explain to Frau Schu-

---

71. The matter of Frau Schumann's copy for Bogler is discussed in letters of 25 June and 1 July 1858 (see *Schumann-Brahms Briefe*, 1:220–25). Friedchen Wagner's account of Brahms's gift for her is quoted in Sophie Drinker, *Brahms and His Women's Choruses* (Merion, Pa., 1952), 74, and reprinted, with revisions from the original typescript in the Drinker Manuscripts at Smith College, Northampton, Mass., in Gotwals, "Brahms and the Organ," 45.

Example 2.15: Brahms, Chorale Prelude on "O Traurigkeit,
o Herzelied," WoO 7 (original version): *a*, mm. 1–3;
b, mm. 11 to end. Reproduced from Johannes Brahms,
Werke für Orgel, with permission of G. Henle Verlag, Munich.

mann the hopeless condition of her husband; the two fugues, with their
suggestive and intertwined evocations of Clara, Robert, and Johannes
himself; the chorale prelude, whose implied text begins by commemo-
rating one person but ends by expressing heartfelt empathy for another – these pieces traverse a difficult and rapidly changing emotional

landscape. At the beginning, the beloved Clara Schumann was a friend's wife; by the end, his widow. And, of course, it soon became clear that Brahms was never to become her husband. The beautiful final measures of "O Traurigkeit," then, seem entirely fitting: they bring poignant closure, not only to a remarkable series of compositions but to a troubled chapter in Brahms's life.

THREE

Contradictory Criteria in a Work of Brahms

Joseph Dubiel

To postpone the first clear presentation of a composition's tonic triad is a characteristic Brahmsian gambit. Troping on the delay of closure, this maneuver delays an aspect of initiation, reaching its point of reference only by way of conclusion. Single-mindedness is not the ideal qualification for appreciating such doings, therefore, despite the crucial importance of holding out for what does not occur. But still less adequate would be the softheadedness that set aside concern for the tonic to go with the flow – because concern for the tonic defines the flow. What is needed depends in part on the nature of the postponement: on what happens until the tonic arrives and how clear the tonic's identity is until then. Sometimes, as in the much discussed Intermezzo in B♭, op. 76, no. 4, a preparatory harmony is elaborated before the tonic; sometimes, as at the equally celebrated opening of the Quintet, op. 115, the subject of elaboration is the process of establishing the tonic, from an initial state of uncertainty about what it is. It can even happen that a section containing no satisfactory tonic triad represents the tonic key relative to some excursion that follows; the startling song "Parole," op. 7, no. 2, is an instance. In such a case, an initial tonic section apparently is to be heard as closed with respect to the excursion, even though still open with respect to its internal activity. More explicitly, such a section's implication of a particular completion causes whatever else it does to sound like a delay of that completion;[1] but then

1. Here I try to be precise about a difference between *implication* and *expectation*: the former concerns reactions to various possible continuations, depending on the degree to which they

something happens that is still not that completion, and the section closes anyway, leaving no obligation for its sequel to provide the implied conclusion. About such things, a responsive listener must be of two minds at least.

Many-mindedness is likewise requisite to the understanding of another phenomenon perhaps equally frequent in Brahms, if less peculiar to him: the use of chromatic motives to establish a sense of voice-leading consecution or harmonic proximity that is at odds with tonal norms. Of this, the most vivid instance may be the motto of the Third Symphony, whose identity, beyond the intervallic succession minor third, major sixth, includes the initial minor third's creating a cross-relation with the harmony supporting the motive's first pitch. Arguably, the full exploration of this facet of the motive gives rise to the first movement's idiosyncratic modulatory plan, which makes something equally idiosyncratic of its form (and has its effect on the other movements). Once again, the full impact of such events depends on a clear idea of what would displace a given note or collection of notes and a successful displacement at odds with this idea.

What links these phenomena, on my account of them, is the operation of two different, and strictly incompatible, criteria for interpreting a span of musical time as open or closed, one of which enjoys the support of the tonal system as the other does not, but the other of which is able to override it, often on a large scale. There are rewards for subscribing to both criteria, meanings to be lost by suspending one or the other. In a nice intensification of what I believe always to be true, the best understanding clearly lies not in the simplest explanation of the data, but in the most complex interpretation of them – which, in these instances, means the maintenance of both sets of interpretive criteria.

Understanding regular contrariety requires a listener to accept as explanatory and referential what is at the same time abnormal. To capture such occurrences' multiplicity of implication, I want to call them *abnorms*: definably irregular events that become criteria of prolongation or succession in violation of larger norms of the pieces in

---

conform to, or extend beyond, the conception of a passage that a listener has formed by the time of their occurrence, but does not entail – as the latter seems to – any laying of odds on these various continuations' likelihood. I understand my distinction between the two to be sharper than the perhaps similarly motivated one expressed by Leonard Meyer in *Explaining Music* (Berkeley: University of California Press, 1973), 114–15n.

which they occur. Abnorms are motives, at least; but they are more, in that *what* they motivate is especially clear because it is importantly unlike "what would have happened" otherwise. Their going against the grain is part of what is motivic about them.

I do not propose to answer general questions about what can be an abnorm, or how an abnorm can be established and resolved, for I see no way for those questions to be smaller than the most general questions of musical reference. I am going to identify a few abnorms in the first movement of Brahms's Piano Concerto in D Minor, op. 15, and discuss the exigencies and rewards of maintaining the many-mindedness that they exact (which is undoubtedly prerequisite to any address to those larger questions).

I

More precise than to say that the appearance of a stable tonic is postponed in the concerto's first movement might be to say that the process of stabilizing the tonic is hugely protracted – arguably until the recapitulation. I split this hair in order to deal with a number of undeniable tonics in the ritornello and exposition, whose stability is qualified by their situation in this process, not by their own features. Some are approached in a manner too little like a resolution of what precedes them, or too little like a cadence, for them to answer every expectation of a tonic; others, though approached impressively, are subsequently swallowed back into the continuing process. A survey of these tonics should clarify my claim.

There is first the opening unharmonized D, which certainly can be heard as a tonic – which, in the long run, must be – but which, on the spot, is the first element to appear of a complex texture, each of whose subsequent elements draws it further from the tonic triad. The B♭ triad that appears in m. 2 can still belong to the D-minor scale and, indeed, still be heard as a D-minor triad modified by an appoggiatura to its fifth. But this and any other diatonic interpretations are brought into question by the A♭ and E♭ that come with the trills of mm. 4ff. The identity of the resulting harmony includes a blatant superimposition of conflicting meanings, "augmented-sixth-chord-elaborated-as-dominant-seventh"; accordingly, its resolution to an A triad "as if its A♭ were G♯" always involves this putative G♯ moving to G♮, as A♭ would, never to A.

There is a near approach to the tonic at the end of the ritornello's first section, in the six-four of m. 25 – more exactly, a near approach to the dominant that should lead to the tonic, itself delayed by the pitch classes of the tonic. This six-four leads into a new section, beginning in the tonic, without benefit of the cadence it implies. The contrabasses hold their low A as the cellos begin an ostinato above it, and then release it, simply uncovering the cellos' D as the lowest pitch. The functional bass remains ambiguous; the six-four is neither resolved nor displaced.

The D-minor triad does occur in root position at the solo entrance in m. 91, but its stability is again compromised by a curious approach to it. Most obviously, its appearance is not the onset of a D root: a D-major triad has been present for some time, so that the piano brings only a slip of mode to minor. Moreover, this D-major triad is strongly inflected as the dominant of G minor, and the modal change recalls an internal event of an earlier theme (the theme introduced by the evaded cadence of mm. 25ff., changing mode in mm. 31–32 and mm. 39–40).[2] This assemblage of adapted obliquities could hardly be better contrived to counter the natural momentousness of the soloist's entrance; and the ecstasy of reticence affects the tonic as well.

Thus is the tonic qualified at two crucial points of articulation: the first large-scale change of any kind, at the end of the ritornello's first section, and the first appearance of the soloist. The right *notes* may be present, but not the functional entity that the B♭ chord supplanted. And each of these is, extraordinarily, the strongest D-minor triad to occur before a change of key — the ritornello's local move to B♭ minor and the exposition's tonicization of F major.

The situation at m. 66, between the ritornello and the exposition, is more complicated. Here D is reached through a cadence, a spectacular one; the qualification of D consists in its immediate reorientation back toward the B♭ chord that initially delayed it – as though the resolution of this chord somehow did not take and the process must be attempted all over again. Most of the orchestra drops out immediately after the downbeat, in a kind of instrumental *forte-piano*, after which the surviving instruments' crescendo transforms the cadential D into the opening D – not merely sustained as the outcome of the cadence, but directed back into the B♭ triad and all that comes with it. By m. 67, then, the chord of the opening seems not to have been conclusively resolved, not even by the forceful cadence of m. 66: it is still there to be dealt with.[3]

2. This affinity between these themes may be heard to permit the replacement of the ritornello theme by the soloist's theme in the recapitulation.

3. The opening music is both louder (*fortissimo*) and more complex (through imitation) on

At the beginning of the recapitulation, the tonic is driven into place by a still more intimidating version of this cadence (mm. 306–10); yet the specter of the B♭ chord arises again at once – due in part precisely to the precedent of mm. 66–67. The piano's E six-four-two in m. 311 is at least as vividly an alternative to the B♭ chord as it is to the tonic, perhaps even more so. In a way this E chord works for the tonic, even as it pushes the tonic aside, because it finally breaks the spell of the B♭ chord.

The shock of this E six-four-two is the effect in which it is most obvious that both the tonic and its regular stand-in are being maintained as norms. The B♭ chord, as pointedly and persistently not the tonic, thus qualifies as my first abnorm. An exception to the tonic, it is also a point of reference – even on the largest scale. This exceptional chord is sometimes even a point of reference for what will eventually resolve it – as at m. 67, where it swallows up the very tonic to which it is an exception. How can I maintain both that the tonic inflects the B♭ chord and that the B♭ chord inflects the tonic?

The answer is by not maintaining both interpretations of the same objects at the same time. My account of m. 66 suggests that its D, as part of the tonic, ends a sixty-six-measure span, while, as part of the B♭ triad, it initiates a later span that directly continues the beginning. So I *am* talking about two things, if I am talking about spans; if I am talking about D, I think my two incompatible things about it at different times. I am not simply calling the D "ambiguous": I *am* ascribing two meanings to it, but not simultaneously and not indifferently to the timing of their onset.[4]

---

its return. If we share Tovey's perception of the opening music as "not represent[ing] a fortissimo at all," but "a sound of distant menace, growing thunderously nearer whenever the harmony changes" (*Essays*, 3:115), then we might well hear this intensified return as continuing the advance – which could leave us with a still stronger sense of the menacing B♭ sonority's having persisted all the while "behind" the ritornello.

4. David Lewin takes a similar line in his provocative "Music Theory, Phenomenology, and Modes of Perception" (*Music Perception* 3 [1986]: 327–92) – may take it further, indeed, insofar as he may incline to exclude the single sonic event from his ontology, in favor of the multiple perceptions of it. I find the starkness of this move (the characteristic move of phenomenology, as I understand it) attractive, but also extravagant and slightly disorienting – chiefly because I am not sure exactly how it provides for those experiences' seeming to be *of* something external (and not a little because, as a composer, I absolutely need those external entities in my ontology). In any event, I do not doubt that Lewin and I are motivated by similar intuitions, and we agree exactly that "to say [two contradictory] things about . . . *two distinct mental objects* (or acts), that is about [two perceptions], is very different from

Example 3.1: Schematic middlegrounds. *a*, Normal. *b*, Abnormal.

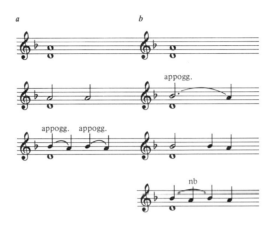

I can make this explicit with the aid of ex. 3.1, which shows two baldly schematic middlegrounds for the beginning of the movement. Example 3.1*a* shows A, the fifth of a D-minor triad, elaborated through re-articulation, and then through embellishment of each resulting A with a B♭ appoggiatura. No relation between the appoggiaturas is asserted by this graph, because they are never shown as belonging to the same span at any level. In ex. 3.1*b* they do belong to one span at the second level: they both derive from a single rearticulated B♭ appoggiatura that is embellished by a neighboring A at the next level. This second graph may seem bizarre – it should, since it is formulated according to abnormal criteria. And I do not propose it as a way of hearing what has happened by the downbeat of m. 66. As far as the two graphs will have been uncovered by that time – I refer just to spans that have been completed – they are the same, and ex. 3.1*a* is a preferable interpretation of the configurations they share because it is supported by the norms of D minor. But when D initiates the B♭ span that groups back over the tonic to the beginning, ex. 3.1*b* takes over. When I say this, I do not mean that ex. 3.1*b* is now the analysis: the analysis is *both* graphs and everything I have just said. I mean only that, within the portion of the piece that ex. 3.1 covers, the criteria represented by ex. 3.1*b* obtain over a longer period of time. Thus the D of m. 66 has two meanings, one of which does not fit very well with D minor and therefore does not come

having to assert that there is *one acoustic object* . . . which 'is' both [one perceptual entity] and [another perceptual entity] at the same time" (p. 353).

up as long as a more normal D-minor interpretation is still possible. The abnormal span is uncovered when the D-minor span inside it ends; but then this span reaches back to the beginning.

When an abnorm regulates succession, the issue of interpretive timing takes a different form. The ritornello's most prominent abnormal succession is C♯'s descent to C♮ every time it appears before the cadence of mm. 64–66 (mm. 21, 35, and 40). To hear C♯ as a leading tone means to be prepared to close a span with D and to hear any other successor as delaying D to keep the span open. To accept C♮ as an abnormal continuation of C♯ is to allow the span of C♯ to close without a D, and thereafter no longer to concern oneself particularly with the prospect of D. A consistent D-minor hearing will normally not entertain the prospect of C♮ as a displacement of C♯ until a C♮ actually appears – and even then only with good reason.

I hope it is clear that to use the notion of abnorms it is necessary not only to interpret the events of a piece but also to specify, for any interpretation that can be contradicted, *when* it becomes relevant and *for how long* it is the leading possibility. This would be a healthy requirement to make of analysis generally, so long as the aim is to describe an experience, rather than merely a "structure."[5]

II

To illustrate, I will offer three accounts of the ritornello, differing in their stance with respect to the two abnorms I have identified. The first will hold close to the most conventional tonal norms, acknowledging the abnorms only as exceptions, however outlandish this may make the passage seem. The second will accept almost anything the passage does as normal; specifically, it will accept the abnorms merely as motives, without making their contradiction of tonal norms any part of their identity. The third analysis will try to accept these contradictions, and to negotiate between them, without denial of their force, through careful attention to the temporal frames of the perceptions they entail.

* * *

5. A powerful statement of this is J. K. Randall's " 'a Soundscroll.' " (*Perspectives of New Music* 13, no. 2 [Spring–Summer 1975]: 126–49), about which commentary can be found in my "Senses of Sensemaking" and Robert Snarrenberg's "Zen and the Way of Soundscroll," both in ". . . Is, with Respect to: Texts and Thoughts in the Space of J. K. Randall" (*Perspectives of New Music* 30, no. 1 [Winter 1992]: 210–21 and 222–37).

For a conventional tonal analysis, the major problem posed by the ritornello is the failure of the tonic six-four in m. 25 to be completed by a dominant and root-position tonic; this is intensified by the absence of any earlier root-position tonic, and compounded by the subsequent turn to B♭ minor, at m. 45, with the question of the tonic still in the air. The point about B♭ minor is not so much that it is an unusual or remote key as that it represents an extraneous issue imposed upon a situation still awaiting completion with respect to an important norm. (This is only more true in a hearing that expects no modulation in this part of the form.) If, after turning away from the urgent business of a tonic cadence, the piece can turn away again like this, then its standards of reasonable progression are not clear. And so the best way to hear the ritornello may be as following a temporarily *un*reasonable progression, whose point is precisely to go out on a limb, and then out further, before the crashing tonic cadence of mm. 64–66 pushes aside the interpolations and returns to the main line of action. Mounting incoherence is eventually redeemed by a stroke of brute force.

Though this interpretation somehow addresses B♭ minor's remoteness, it still leaves that remoteness essentially indiscriminate: B♭ minor is just some distant key. To connect it to the irregular B♭ chord of the opening is tempting, but problematic. For one thing, the B♭ triad is elusive at the beginning: at first a modified D-minor triad, soon after part of the intensely ambiguous seventh chord I have described. Even if it can be retrieved as a B♭-major triad, it does little to suggest B♭ minor as a later tonic. For another, the tonic triads in the B♭-minor section are inconspicuous and unhelpful: there are none in root position, nor any disposed as F–B♭ over D♭ so as to invoke the opening six-three. The connection between this section's tonic and the opening chord lies mostly in the label "B♭."

In truth, this reservation applies as well to the very identification of this section with its ostensible tonic of B♭ minor. The section's characteristic sonority is the dominant – especially the dominant-ninth chord produced by retaining the diminished-seventh of mm. 41–44 over a bass F. The B♭-minor section does not resolve the diminished-seventh that precedes it, but retains it and gives it a new tonal interpretation. Examined in this modest degree of detail, then, the B♭-minor section seems still less stable than it did in my outline of the ritornello: it dangles from the diminished-seventh chord at the end of the section before.

And this diminished-seventh itself is only loosely attached to what precedes *it*. The section that it ends begins by carrying on the harmonic action of the opening section, as I have described, taking over m. 25's six-four as the harmony of its first phrase and resolving it to the dominant at the end of the phrase in m. 34. The cello ostinato retains the sound of the six-four after the basses release low A – along with a motivic relation to the beginning (shown in ex. 3.2)[6] – and low A is explicitly reasserted in m. 31 to preserve the six-four through the change of mode. The section's second phrase, since it does not resolve the dominant with which the first phrase ends, must extend it. The change to minor mode in m. 35 undermines the dominant's cadential implications, however, and the second phrase gradually proves to parallel the first one, in A minor. So the dominant of m. 34, far from being prolonged by the second phrase, falls into place as transitional to it. It is clear at this point that the important concerns of m. 25 have been suspended, to be recovered in an as yet unknown way at an unknown time. If it is not clear just *when* they are suspended – m. 35, or m. 27, or somewhere in between – then this only makes the situation at the end of the section more heavily loaded, and therefore less hospitable to the diminished-seventh chord – and much less hospitable to B♭ minor.

Example 3.2: Motivic relation between opening melody and cello ostinato.

The diminished-seventh chord, then, advances neither the second section's inherited purposes nor its independent ones: it turns away from both. But B♭ minor cannot explain this chord, either: in its remoteness, this key depends on the diminished-seventh chord to account for *it*. We cannot have it both ways. Thus the diminished-seventh chord is

---

6. On the basis of this connection (and, presumably, the key scheme), Tovey assimilates this section to the first one, saying that "its [the first section's] climax subsides into a mournful cantabile, accompanied by its ubiquitous main figure," and reserving talk of "a new theme" for the third section (*Essays*, 3:115–16).

unavoidably a turn away from the second section's action, compounding the perversity of evading the six-four; and the third section prolongs the resulting bewilderment until the music of the first section closes around it all at m. 64.

Compared to this analysis, the second will start with few presuppositions. It will not go so far as to abandon the search for a satisfactory tonic, but it will see a more plausible candidate in the D-minor triad of m. 25, and not hold out for a specific further completion of it as the first analysis did.

This single relaxation improves the continuity of the ritornello in a number of respects. Most obviously, it leaves the second section freer to turn to the diminished-seventh chord. There may still be no positive reason to go there; but there are at least fewer reasons not to, once the imposition of the six-four is lightened. From the viewpoint of the second section, the effective bass note after m. 26 doesn't even *have* to be A: if it is D, then both the section's phrases are alike in moving their tonic triads from five-three to six-four position. Thus it need not be the six-four in particular, with all its demands, that the second section continues from m. 25, but just the D-minor triad, as a long awaited collection of pitch classes.

Any indulgence toward six-fours also improves the status of B♭ minor: the bass F is no longer such a problem, and may even be an advantage, since it can admit B♭ to the company of the other local tonics inclined to six-four position. Moreover, to identify B♭ minor strongly with this bass F is implicitly to relate it more closely to the tonic triad of the movement, to which F of course belongs. The better F sounds, the more the third section can be *about* F rather than about the diminished-seventh, and so the more stable it can be relative to the diminished-seventh.

At this point the second analysis offers more solutions than there ever were problems: the diminished-seventh is, if not less mysterious on the spot, at least less contrary; and the B♭-minor music nonetheless has more to add by way of explanation.

And still there is more to be said for B♭ minor. Just as six-four position is more normal in this context than in tonal music at large, so may minor mode be, on similar grounds – namely, that it is common to all the local tonics of the ritornello. It may matter more that the key of B♭ match the other two keys in mode than that it match the B♭-major triad that occurs in the D-minor scale. This, too, would lessen the strangeness of B♭ minor. It would also overcome an impediment to the association between B♭ minor and the B♭ major of the opening, provided that this association be made by way of the explicit *changes* of mode that the D and A triads undergo in the second section. The B♭ triad responds to these changes by changing its mode, to minor, between its appearance at the beginning and its appearance as local tonic in the third section. To press this somewhat extravagant claim I must show how to recover a B♭ triad from the opening, despite the dim view of my chances given in the first analysis.

To hear the B♭ triad requires making a sharp division between the arpeggiation in mm. 2–3 and the trill figure that follows; this division is coextensive with the one between pure triad and hard-to-interpret seventh chord, and remains so whenever these motives are in play. In the second version of this material, in mm. 11–20, the analogous moment is marked by a break in melodic parallelism to the first version and by a reimposition of B♭ upon the A triad. The continuously dissonant chords of the rest of the section are expressed by unbroken strings of trills. And finally it is just the arpeggiating figure that becomes the triadic ostinato of mm. 25ff.

The division of the opening melody into arpeggiation and trills does more for the connection to B♭ minor than allow the B♭-major triad to be recovered; for the three triads graced with the arpeggiating figure in the span from the beginning to the onset of the ostinato – B♭ in mm. 2–3, A in mm. 12–13, and D in mm. 25ff. – are precisely the three that become local tonics in the ritornello and that undergo changes of mode.

This rehabilitation of B♭ minor gives grounds for a new account of the ritornello's continuity. If B♭ minor is intelligible as a place to go for its own sake, it can certainly absorb the diminished-seventh chord as locally transitional to it. In a broader sense, the entire second section can be heard to effect a transition between the first and the third – by being soft like the third section but still close to the first section's key of D minor, and by preparing B♭'s change of mode.

This preparation involves not only the simple setting of a precedent with D and A, but also a melodic detail. The D and A triads' changes of mode include direct successions of these triads' major and minor thirds: F♯–F♮ in m. 32 and C♯–C♮ in m. 40. The second of these, C♯–C♮, leads into the diminished-seventh chord of mm. 41–44, by the end of which it will become the D♭–C of B♭ minor. It is followed in mm. 41–42 by an ambiguous dyad written, and eventually heard, as G♭–F (which

clearly has F♯–F♮ as its most relevant precursor), and then by the ubiquitous B♭–A. And these three dyads, D♭–C, G♭–F, and B♭–A, together
define the B♭-harmonic-minor scale in the same sidelong way in which
the opening's B♭ and A triads define the D-minor. Moreover, the two of
these dyads produced by enharmonic reinterpretation become salient
details of the third section – G♭–F the defining feature of the dominant-
ninth, D♭–C the melodic wrinkle of m. 47 and many parallel places. In
short, the move to B♭ minor draws on particulars of D's and A's changes
of mode, as well as on the precedent they provide. Meanwhile, the
analogy of approach to a minor key through VI and V triads sharpens
the sense of B♭ minor as counterpole to the opening in the large progression of the ritornello.

The enharmonic change of C♯ to D♭ is explicitly undone near the end
of the ritornello, with the enharmonic equivalent of a B♭-minor triad,
C♯–F–B♭, formed in passing within the C♯ diminished-seventh chord of
mm. 62–63. The same diminished-seventh chord is then superimposed
over F in the first loud chord of m. 64. This chord recalls the same
diminished-seventh chord at m. 14 in the first section, which I have
already mentioned as a lapse in parallelism between the opening's first
two phrases; the moment matters here as a literal extension of B♭ over
C♯, and so as the first section's nearest approach to combining B♭ with
D♭. Thus, even this aspect of B♭ minor's relation to the opening is not
utterly far-fetched.

Meanwhile the bass F of m. 64 participates in an even neater and
more comprehensive undoing of the ritornello's action. This analysis,
by making six-four chords a little less shaky, and by allowing mm. 41–44
to be a transition, has produced the overall bass line of D to A for the
first section, reflected again in the first phrase of the second section and
imitated A to E in the second phrase, followed, after the transition, by F
in the third section. Now, starting from the F of m. 64, the bass line of
the cadence reverses this: F–E–A–A–D (see ex. 3.3).

It is appropriate that this cadence should be so influenced by what has
happened since the first section, since in this analysis that action is much
more coherent and directed, less an interruption, than in the first analysis. What I have just said about the cadence is only the last touch in a
picture that has been developing for some time: in contrast to the first
analysis's sense of each section as uneasily dependent on the one before,
until the cadence intervenes, this analysis portrays the first and third
sections as two well-defined and comparable points connected by the

Example 3.3: Ritornello's bass summarized.

second section. The transitional second section begins by taking over the tonic triad from the first and worrying over its bass position to make its own tune and then gives itself over to the third section by preparing B♭ minor through the mode changes of the tonic and dominant triads.

* * *

In place of a vague and shifting sense of what might depend on what, and at the expense only of a few apparently irrelevant rigidities, the second analysis offers a step-by-step progression along a reasonable, if idiosyncratic, path to a distant place, followed by a summary return to the starting point. On the face of it, then, the second analysis is more successful than the first. It does not leave so many passages interrupted and unable to influence the music that interrupts them, and it uncovers a rich and intricate motivic network that would be relatively inaccessible from a more tonal point of view. Yet there are virtues of the first analysis worth keeping – foremost among them the very sense of mounting complication through the ritornello that has been so hard to describe coherently. Under the second interpretation the passage's continuity is tamer and more conventional (or at least its unconventionality is not represented as part of its sound). Also desirable is the intensity of the first reading's concern with the tonic triad; for without this, the subsequent qualified tonics (of mm. 66 and 91) will do at least as well as the tonic of m. 25, and the large-scale drama of working toward a stronger tonic will collapse. Finally, there is the simple fact of the first analysis *being* so "tonal," and thereby keeping the concerto in a literature to which it seems to belong.

My response to this dilemma is conditioned by a fundamental analytical avarice: the wish to ascribe as much meaning as possible to the piece, and as much as possible to work this meaning into my hearing – to make it *perceived* meaning. This attitude dictates an effort to combine the analyses. The problematic point for such a combination is of course the tonic six-four of m. 25, where the second analysis happily ends a span and the first doggedly keeps one open. On the basis of this difference, utterly dissimilar continuities arise: in the first hearing, increasingly perilous attenuation of connection to this preoccupying point, saved in the nick of time; in the second, two distantly but rationally related regions connected by an elegant and surprising transition. Pluralist though I may wish to be – pluralist though I know how to be with regard to the six-four sonority   I would find the simultaneous assertion of these two progressions virtually unintelligible. If both these hearings can be managed at once, then I don't know what two interpretations of a musical passage ever couldn't be maintained together, and I simply don't know how to proceed.

To make this combination of perceptions intelligible to myself, it helps to use the C♯–C♮ abnorm, with the temporal care I have described. This abnorm gives me a way to hear the dominant of m. 34 – that is, the resolution of the six-four of m. 25 – as satisfactorily displaced by something other than a tonic. As a matter of mere motivic connection, invoking the fall of C♯ to C♮ in m. 21 as a precedent for the fall of C♯ to C♮ in m. 35 smacks of note-picking, since the dynamic, phraseological, and harmonic settings of the two moves differ by about as much as is consistent with the presence of the same two pitch classes. But in relation to the usual implications of a leading tone, the two moves have more in common: precisely their abnormality. Each deflects a possible tonic resolution of a long anticipated dominant. In the terms of my earlier discussion of abnorms, this means that, although C♯ may fall to C♮ each time, the larger norms of D minor will suggest its resolution to D until the last possible moment – and will not be wrong, for a time span that ends, each time, with C♮'s appearance. As I said in connection with ex. 3.1, C♯'s abnormal meaning is associated with a longer span of time that is uncovered only when the shorter span inside it ends.

For the first section of the ritornello, the action of the longer span is the chromatic passing motion from D down to A; the immediate prospect for C♯, prior to m. 21, is a return to D, which seems especially timely after a monstrous chord has forced the first tonic note of the piece to resolve to its leading tone. It is not that the tonic must (or should) come next, but only that no other prospect is nearly as well defined through

m. 20. To put it simply, there is no reason to think of C♯ as a passing tone: a passing tone is something it becomes when C♮ follows it.[7]

When the sense of a long passing motion imposes itself on the opening, something else important follows: the first chord extends its influence over the entire span. No longer is the chord over D resolved by the chord over C♯; instead there is an unarticulated motion down from D, prolonging the harmony that appeared over D, through its brief recurrence in the latter half of m. 24, until its displacement to the six-four over A in m. 25. The continuing influence of the most problematic form of the chord is luridly manifested all the way to that goal by the trills on the most problematic pitch classes associated with it, B♭, E♭, and A♭ (in mm. 14–19, 21–22, and 23). The two abnorms thus cooperate: it is when the C♯–C♮ move displaces the dominant that the first section can take on the aspect of an elaboration, through passing motion, of the B♭ chord. The relation of long-range displacement between the B♭ chord and the tonic six-four is microscopically reflected in the single pitch-class change that takes place between the initial arpeggiation and the cello ostinato: the resolution at last of B♭ to A. (Example 3.2 can be read for this change.)

Although I think of my third analysis as essentially the first analysis improved by an admixture of abnormal elements from the second, I do wish to qualify slightly its insistence on the six-four at the beginning of the second section. I have already seen to it that the six-four-to-dominant interpretation of the phrase will not be left a loose end, but I wish also to leave room for the second analysis's recognition of the two parallel phrases changing their triads from five-three to six-four position.

Such a qualification illuminates the character of the passage, which could have been contrived precisely to prolong uncertainty as to which attributes of the first section persist. This uncertainty is objectivized in the cello ostinato, whose motivic relation to the opening tune is two-edged in a way I have so far slighted: to speak only of "derivation" does not capture the difference between the opening proclamation and a

7. In response to the objection that the chromatic descent from tonic to dominant is a minor-mode topic that an informed listener fully anticipates, at least as early as D's fall to C♯, I would suggest that Brahms (who undoubtedly knew the ins and outs of elaborating this progression) inhibits this anticipation by making the leading tone a *resolution* of the dissonant tonic note; after the leading tone descends, I would be inclined to agree that further descent to the dominant emerges as a clear prospect.

low murmur that sounds like an accompaniment even before there is anything for it to accompany. It is hard to say whether such a transformation really makes for a sense of close continuation of the former event by the latter; it may equally suggest that the change from one to the other is categorical.

The tune, for its part, enters almost as an aspect of the ostinato; and even once its presence can no longer be denied, the more distinctive of its two intertwined voice-leading strands, the F–E–F♯ of mm. 27, 29, and 31, which brings the phrase's characteristic change of mode, is slow to assert itself against the motivically well-connected A–B♭ of mm. 28 and 30. The highlight of F♯ can color m. 31's six-four in two ways: either as an explicit reappearance of a sonority present all along, or as the return of a sonority temporarily displaced.

In all these respects, then, there simply is no telling whether the first phrase prolongs the six-four of m. 25, or resolves it and then presents a new one; in this instance it is particularly clear that "prolongation" is a way of listening – a matter of how hard I choose to hold on to the six-four.[8] One way or another, it eventually comes about that a six-four resolves to a root-position dominant, and that all of the first phrase becomes a model for the second. After m. 35, the phrases' common pattern is revealed to be more or less what the second analysis said it was – except that, thanks to the abnorm C♯–C♮, the second phrase's continuation of the dominant entails neither a decline in the dominant's status nor the sense of a random turn taken.

The second section's evasion of D minor is facilitated by the association between C♮ in m. 35 and C♮ in m. 21, an association perceptibly largely by virtue of both C♮s' succeeding C♯s, contrary to the ordinary demands of D minor. The reinforcement of this connection by the inclusion of abnormality in the motive's definition provides the most concrete illustration of why I want to maintain this sort of double reference. It shows how much would be left unsaid by the mere identification of C♯–C♮ as "motivic," without a sense of that motive as contrary to a norm, or by the mere addition to this account of a comment about C♯–C♮'s infrequency in tonal practice. My purpose is to insist on an account of what happens when the sense of an event's being unusual is worked into the hearing of a piece, not left as a matter of collateral music-

---

8. For some more general thoughts on this subject, see my " 'When You Are a Beethoven': Kinds of Rules in Schenker's *Counterpoint*" (*Journal of Music Theory* 34 [1990]: 291–340).

historical reflection. And I think that the essential technical requirement for that is to follow out the chronology of the interaction of two
contrary norms. Insofar as I have a methodological point to make in
this section, I have made it.

To finish my account of the ritornello – insofar as this is my point – I
must make good my neglect of the third C♯–C♮ move, the one in mm.
39–41, which I have so far assimilated to the one in mm. 34–35. It is, of
course, the reassertion of minor mode that regularly follows the momentary major of this tune; but it deserves special attention for the
way it resolves the harmonic discrepancy between the A-minor triad of
m. 35 and the diminished-seventh chord of m. 21 – by ushering in the
enharmonic equivalent of that diminished-seventh chord in m. 41. This
move thus more explicitly recaptures the context of the first C♯–C♮
move in m. 21 than the A-minor triad does; and it to some extent cures
the lingering unattached quality of the A-minor triad in this analysis
by making it a step toward the return of the diminished-seventh in
the transition and in the B♭-minor section. I have already described the
B♭-minor section as responsive, in several aspects of its thematic substance, to lines of development toward B♭ minor, and can now add that
its initial melodic descent from E♭ alludes to a salient feature of mm.
21ff.

These same considerations help to recover some of the first analysis's
sense of the B♭-minor section not completely displacing the diminished-
seventh chord, but without the same puzzlement about the chord itself.
They also suggest again a sense of the second section almost coming
apart in the middle: in particular they create a span beginning with the
C♯–C♮ move of mm. 34–35, continuing through a better approximation
of C♮'s original harmonic context in m. 40, and following into that
chord's fuller reinterpretation in the third section. Though this span
may cut across obvious thematic divisions, it is marked with the unique
use of violin mutes in the movement.

III

This close study of the ritornello may make it credible that these abnorms are more than ordinary motives, but I can indicate their full
scope only by projecting them forward through the first movement
(and a little beyond). In particular, I need to show how they eventually
"resolve," how their conflict with tonal norms is alleviated – an issue
that would never arise for ordinary motives. The B♭ abnorm is fully itself

only if it forces together the sound of a dominant-seventh and that of an augmented-sixth, and especially if it stands in for the tonic of D minor; and the C♯–C♮ abnorm is fully itself only if it deflects the leading tone, preferably of a long anticipated dominant, and especially if it defers a cadence to the tonic. These attributes do not always travel with the notes B♭ and C♯–C♮, however; in fact, they increasingly tend not to as the movement goes on, particularly in the recapitulation and coda. It makes sense that this should happen, if the sense is assimilation of the abnorms to background norms.

I will first describe the abnorms' involvement in the major action of the exposition, namely the tonicization of F major for the second group of themes, in which context I will suggest that the tonicization's seeming "motivated" is largely a matter of F major's providing a frame within which the succession D–C♯–C♮, reinterpreted as D–D♭–C♮, sheds much of its contrariety. This reminder of abnormality as definitive of abnorms will then provide a standpoint for describing their resolution in the recapitulation, notably in their interaction with the tonic's change from minor mode to major; and this in turn will permit a few observations of the development and coda, and of the concerto's other two movements.

* * *

In the exposition, the second group's major mode sets it apart from all the preceding tonics, creating a greater change than even the ritornello's far-fetched B♭ minor. Yet the tonic F begins, like all the others, in the minor mode, and even with an old theme, the one introduced in B♭ minor. The dominant pedal that characterizes this theme is C; and the modulation from D to F is accomplished by a chromatic descent to this C from D. This descent evokes the abnormal succession D–C♯–C♮, but lessens its abnormality, for C♯ is reinterpreted as D♭ before it falls to C♮. The modulation to some degree domesticates the abnormal voice leading, directing both D♮ and D♭ toward C♮; and the difference between D♮ and D♭, as symptomatic of the difference between major and minor modes, is then thematic throughout the second group.

The chromatic descent begins from the exposition's initial D, which does not move before its music is cut off at m. 76. C♯ follows when this music is resumed at m. 110 – with E, G, and B♭ established above it before A is, in contrast to its original harmonization. This theme's ordinary course, now resumed, leads again to a six-four in m. 117, which (after elaboration begun by a resurgent B♭ chord in m. 118) resolves to the dominant in m. 123, leaving the next theme to move from A to E (rather than from D to A). Accordingly, the end of the second theme reassembles E, G, and B♭ in m. 136; the diminished-seventh chord of m. 110 is completed by a fourth note, precedented as C♯ and moving as D♭ (like F♯/G♭ at m. 41) – that is, falling to C♮ immediately in m. 137 and again at the end of the bass arpeggiation B♭–G–E–D♭ in mm. 140–41. And this C♮ is the dominant of F minor.

The change to F major is brought about (between mm. 149 and 150) by a subtly relevant detail: the piano changes C's upper neighboring note from D♭ to D♮, to which the orchestra responds with major-mode reminiscences of the F-minor music, in which D♮ again and again replaces F minor's diagnostic D♭. Within F major, the bass C's first motion is to D♮ (m. 152), contrasting the D♭ from which it came; eventually, this takes its place as a passing tone within the dominant, but on the spot its harmonization is a nice touch: upon the "deceptive resolution" of the dominant to a VI (i.e., D-minor) five-three, it imposes the "extra" deception of a IV (i.e., B♭), thus reproducing not only the pitch classes but surprisingly much of the meaning of the abnormal B♭ triad.

The identification of the two modes on F with the two versions of the sixth degree resonates through the remainder of the exposition. The major articulation within the F-major anthem (mm. 157ff.) is a woodwind excursion to and from the region of ♭VI (mm. 176ff.), easy to hear as D♭–C writ large – and relevantly introduced by the piano's depression of D♮ to D♭ in mm. 172–75. The more agitated passage adumbrating the horn theme (mm. 192ff.) is contrastingly on the D♮, "major" side, set into motion by C♯ (which is succeeded by both D and C♮).[9] The piano's two answers to the horn call (in mm. 199ff.) also gesture in both directions, although, appropriately, not symmetrically: D♮ is unprepossessing in the first of these utterances, which serves as an ordinary major-side foil to the second, whose F minor expands hugely toward D♭ major. The codetta's major-mode recollection of the F-minor music (mm. 216ff.) includes the theme also at its original transpositional level – that is, the

9. The measures leading to this sequence present an astonishing welter of harmonic allusion to the opening: D minor to B♭ major, acquiring a minor seventh in m. 189; this resolving, as a dominant-seventh, to an E♭-major triad, whose juxtaposition with the dominant of F major in m. 190 confronts us with E♭–E♮, the F-major analogue of C♮–C♯; which analogy we can experience directly as m. 191 tears its way from a C-major to an A-major triad – by way of a B♭-major triad.

level associated with B♭ minor – where the change to major is once more a matter of D♮'s replacing D♭; and still D♮'s final descent to C is through D♭.

* * *

When the recapitulation replaces the B♭ chord with an E six-four-two, it contributes to the resolution of this abnorm more significantly than by simple removal of it. The rules of progression change as well: for the first time, the initial harmony of the theme progresses "normally," exactly according to the functional implications in terms of which it is elaborated.[10] Moreover, it is now the E six-four-two, not the B♭ six-three, that the following A harmony takes as a model, both in its initial bass position and in the diminished-fifth skip during its elaboration (D–G♯, m. 317; G♮–C♯, m. 327). These rearrangements make the bass succession G♯–G♮ across the change of harmony (m. 320) a motivic forerunner to the abnormal succession C♯–C♮ (m. 330), so that the bass is unmistakably back on track only when C♮ falls to B♮ (m. 332). With B♮ thus marked, and reinforced by the changed opening chord, there is little to lift the ensuing B♭ (m. 333) above its passing status: no longer does B♭ reproduce the theme's first harmony on the way to its resolution – in fact, B♮ now comes closer to doing so, and B♭'s effect is at most that of a passing reference. After this, the emphatic six-four reached in m. 334 is less vulnerable than it once might have been to displacement by the abnormal chord's return in m. 335. In the ensuing melee, B♭ quickly returns to B♮, whose resolution to A produces a second, bigger crash on the six-four in m. 341. And although this will not come to cadence without further incident – surprises await at m. 345, and even earlier – its difficulties no longer have anything to do with B♭.

The recapitulatory resolution of C♯–C♮ involves *only* a change in the rules, not any elimination of the succession: in the approach to the recapitulation (mm. 306–10), C♯–C♮ is absorbed into the very cadential progression that it usually disrupts. The C♯ of the dominant triad falls to C♮ in m. 307 without incapacitating the dominant; instead, the succession takes its place in an inner-voice descent concatenating the chro-

10. On the one occasion when the B♭ dominant-seventh in this position does not resolve as an augmented-sixth – the interruption of the theme at m. 76 in the exposition – it resolves as a 7–6 suspension, A♭ delaying G over B♭.

matically filled fourth from D down to A and the diatonically filled fifth from A down to D. This line integrates the abnorm into a D-minor framework about as securely as can be imagined.

In the D-major framework established in the recapitulation of the F-major music (mm. 381ff.), it would be easy for both abnorms simply to disappear, since both involve pitch classes foreign to D major. But on the contrary, both the B♭-major triad and the voice-leading succession C♯–C♮ remain conspicuous, and their resolution is a matter of their becoming less disruptive. The major-mode music's turns to ♭VI now are to the B♭-major triad – notably in the woodwind episode of mm. 400ff. and the piano's response to the second horn call beginning in m. 428. (A systematic felicity is that virtually every event in the exposition's F-major music that referred to C♯–C♮, by way of D–D♭–C, now becomes a reference to B♭.) Meanwhile, C♯–C♮ occurs repeatedly, usually in the context D–C♯–C♮–B♭: permeating the second half of the first phrase (mm. 383–84), implicit in the piano's adumbration of the horn call (mm. 390 ff.), and gently drawing out the horn's farewell in mm. 436–37. (A one-of-a-kind felicity is that the explicit linear successions D–C♯–C♮–B of mm. 383–84 occur within an E dominant-seventh applied to the dominant of D – the harmony that replaced the B♭ chord at the beginning of the section.)

But while the B♭ triad and C♯–C♮ remain present as *motives*, they are not clearly influential as *abnorms*. They do not disrupt strongly implied progressions within the D-major music, nor do they present knots of multiple incompatible meanings. In the D–C♯–C♮–B successions of mm. 383–84, neither C♯ nor C♮ is ever a chord tone; they are born passing. In mm. 391–92, the *succession* C♯–C♮ never occurs in any voice: C♯ rises to D in an inner voice, while C♮ embellishes B in the bass. In mm. 436–37, C♯–C♮ occurs in passing over a tonic pedal that lasts from m. 434 through m. 442. Similarly, the woodwinds' B♭ passage is prepared and resolved so that the chord's characteristically superimposed dominant-seventh and augmented-sixth functions are successive: in m. 399, the piano chromatically closes the diminished third G♯–B♭, allowing the woodwinds to begin m. 400 with a pure B♭-major triad and elaborate it into an applied dominant-seventh, which they resolve as an augmented-sixth in m. 406. In the horn-call passage (mm. 428ff.) the abnormal chord's intensity declines further: the chord acquires no A♭, avails itself of a clear momentary G♯ to resolve to a D-minor triad (m. 431), and is finally connected to the dominant by an applied E

JOSEPH DUBIEL

dominant-seventh – which is to say by the very harmony that supplants it at the beginning of the recapitulation.

As invoked in the D-major music, then, both abnorms shed much of their abnormality; their multiple meanings are separated and resolved. In particular, C♯–C♮ ceases to be a deflection of the leading tone, and the B♭ chord ceases to delay the tonic, or to superimpose contrasting harmonic functions. In a manner of speaking, these elements recur only as shadows of their original selves once the recapitulation arrives in D major.

As I have already suggested, the embedding of the abnorms in D major brings out a similarity between them that would not emerge in D minor, namely that they both involve "lowered" forms of scale degrees. This relation comes clear not in the treatment of B♭ and C♮ in the D-major music so much as in the "correction" of them to B♮ and C♯ that brings about the recapitulation's change of mode (mm. 345–80). Compared to what *could* have changed the mode, simply and with precedent – a D-minor version of the ritornello's third theme, changing directly to major, just as in the exposition – the actual approach to major is roundabout. The theme occurs (beginning in m. 366), but in F♯ minor, which key is the outcome of a sequence taking the piano's entrance music from the tonic (six-four) in m. 341 up through a series of major seconds: to E minor in m. 348 and F♯ minor in m. 355. To hear this sequence as *aiming* for F♯ minor is implausible: as with the ritornello's B♭ minor, nothing encourages anticipation of this particular remote key, and the local changes of key are too sudden and surprising to organize the passage. The sequence sounds more like a string of singularities: a deflection of the blockbuster cadence that could conclude the D-minor passage, leaving the tune somehow in E minor, where, of all things, the deflection repeats itself, leading to F♯ minor, where the process stops.[11]

What undermines the D-minor cadence is, first, a disconcerting loss of sound in the preceding two measures (mm. 343–44), and, second, a major triad at the arrival (m. 345) – upon which are rapidly superimposed a minor seventh and a minor ninth, producing the diminished-seventh consistently associated with C♮ abnormally succeeding C♯. The passage thereby presents a step-by-step explanation of how this diminished-seventh chord might come to follow a cadential domi-

11. Tovey seems to share a sense of these modulations as fantastic, writing that "magnificent new harmonic vistas are revealed" (*Essays*, 3:117).

{102}

nant (comparable to the step-by-step explanation of the B♭ chord that follows in the D-major music).[12] As always, this chord's origin implies resolution to the subdominant, with C♮ presumably falling to B♭; but B♮ appears (in m. 347), and the key of E minor suddenly forms around it for the orchestra's rendition of the piano's entrance music.

The cadence that would settle this new key goes just the same way: the cadential triad turns up major and becomes a diminished-seventh that is suddenly redirected toward F♯ minor by an insinuating C♯. As little motivated as the slip to E minor may have been, an imitation of it is still less so – and thus does F♯ minor seem the outcome of a series of surprises more than the target of a progression. On the other hand, the woodwinds' display of C♯ in mm. 354–55 and the piano's reclamation of its tune at least do something to mark F♯ minor *as* the outcome. F♯ minor's C♯, "correct" for D major, meaningfully contrasts F minor's C♭ in the exposition, as though arresting chromatic descent from D before it becomes abnormal.[13] But the replacement of B♭ by B♮ is the crucial change that sets off the entire chain of events.[14] In all, the passage is nicely wrought to be identified neither with E minor, the first key to which it turns, nor with F♯ minor, the last key that it reaches. Both these keys' diagnostic pitch classes, B♮ and C♯, do away with scale degrees – and abnorms – associated with D minor, in preparation for the D-major idyll.

Just conceivably, the establishment of C♯ should be considered the modulating passage's main assignment because so much work is done on B♮ at the beginning of the recapitulation. In a sense, the suppression of B♭ begins even in the development section. The assumption necessary to this interpretation is that the development elaborately reenacts the

12. Meanwhile, the dominant-seventh is also what would come next in a sequence initiated by the recapitulation's first two harmonies.

13. Strenuous *Fernhören* might even reconstitute the modulatory sequence's initial D dominant-seventh (m. 345) as an augmented-sixth, retrospectively orienting the passage toward F♯ minor after all. The reinterpretation of C♮ as B♯, directed toward C♯, through this doubling of harmonic meaning, would allude to both abnorms at once.

14. This transformation of C♯'s diminished-seventh by B♮ (m. 347) complements is transformation by F in the ritornello (mm. 42ff.), suggesting a comparison between the ritornello's turn to B♭ minor, cued by its initial B♭ chord, and the recapitulation's to E minor, cued by its initial E chord. Of the various reinforcements that sustained this admittedly tenuous connection in the original instance, the most crucial, the separation of the initial triad from the dominant-seventh chord, is provided immediately after the E-minor tune (m. 352).

ritornello's initial chromatic descent from D to A, using all (and only) the ritornello's themes – indeed, completes this descent successfully for the first time, ending in the cadential dominant that this descent has always promised, and permitting the recapitulation's escape from the abnorms. This account is recommended by the events of mm. 229–31, where D is recovered and made the bass of the opening theme's B♭ chord, and m. 237, where D falls to C♯, more or less as it always does. What happens next is less straightforward: the bass falls *through* C♮ to B♮ in mm. 243–44,[15] but this B♮ initiates a passage of harmonic wrestling between B♮ and C♮ (articulated by a sequence starting on C♮ in m. 248 and by the elaboration of a diminished-seventh chord including B♮ starting in m. 251),[16] which leads at last to the ritornello's second theme in A minor, with C♮ in the bass, in m. 259. The third section of the development, using the third theme of the ritornello, is in B♭ minor, beginning at m. 278; although this theme does not establish its tonic in the bass at once, B♮ arrives after a strong cadence in m. 287. The moment is further articulated by a change of mode to major, the understated inclusion of a form of the opening motive (in pizzicato violas), and a chromatic descent from the tonic (like that of the opening theme) implicit in the harmony.

With a large-scale bass of D–C♯–C♮–B♮ so easy to recover, and with a pedal on A concluding the section (beginning in m. 295), it seems obvious what to look for in between: a colossal elaboration of a bass B♭ and decisive resolution of it at last to a cadential dominant. But this is exactly what doesn't happen – and at several levels the B♮ passage goes out of its way to make sure it doesn't. First, its bass moves back *up* from B♮ in m. 287 to C♮ in m. 291, with the same tune a minor second higher (the change achieved by the motivically significant arrest of B major's chromatic descent at ♭VI – B♮–A♯–A♮–G♯–G♮). Then, at the last moment

15. This early descent of C♯ to C♮, under the E, G, and B♭ that belong to C♯ (m. 243), creates a tangle of backward references: to D♭–C under E, G, and B♭, accomplishing the main modulation in the exposition; to the initial harmony's typical elaboration as dominant-seventh and resolution as augmented-sixth; and to the bass succession B♮–B♭–A under A♭, becoming G♯, resolving to A, at the end of the first section of the ritornello (mm. 23–25), now exactly paralleled by C♯–C♮–B♮ under B♭, becoming A♯, resolving to B.

16. By the logic of the sequence, the bass note in m. 251 is G♯; but the ornamentation of it by G♮ raises the question of its being A♭ instead – at once reasserting this pitch class's chronic ambiguity, invoking m. 24's B♮–B♭ under A♭/G♯, and in general suggesting the B♭ abnorm in a scene overtly dominated by C♯–C♮ (to which, indeed, G♯–G♮ makes yet another analogy).

of the C-major version (m. 293), the tune's pattern is broken to bring D minor into reach (specifically to set up a bass B♭ in the second half of m. 294, to fall to A in m. 295), and then its new pattern is broken by a G interposed between B♭ and A. This weakens the connection to A of a short bass B♭ that happens in the first place only through a deviation from a pattern, which pattern's very occurrence prevents an imaginable long B♭ from occurring.

What is the point of keeping B♭–A out of the bass of the development? Most obviously, to take a firm line on what will count as resolving the B♭ abnorm – that is, to resolve the chord in its capacity as a substitute for the tonic, by replacing it at the beginning of the recapitulation, rather than merely in its capacity as a colorful preparatory harmony to the dominant. If the move B♭–A were accomplished on the way to the development's final dominant and the succession C♯–C♮ absorbed by this dominant, then the abnorms would be taken care of *before* the recapitulation – and the B♭ chord would have been resolved merely as an approach to the dominant instead of as a challenge to the tonic.

Beyond this, there is considerable point in moving B♭–A to the *treble*: there, it can still belong to the chromatic descent from D to A that resolves C♯–C♮ in mm. 306ff. In the considerable expanse of pedal A that precedes this crucial passage, both abnorms are at work in something like their original forms (except for the pedal). Twice C♮s draw down C♯s, in m. 297 and again in m. 301, each time putting off a cadential dominant with a web of chromatically descending lines; each time, the cadential dominant is brought back within reach by a B♭ chord – only an approximation of the abnorm the first time, in m. 299, but a reproduction of it in m. 304, leading through a six-four to the successful cadential dominant.

But the largest issue – and one in which the development acts well in advance of any likelihood of our hearing what it's about – is the movement's gradual shift out of the minor mode into the major. This line of action is easiest to follow in the tonal career of the movement's most mobile theme, the ritornello's third, the one whose occurrence in B♮ minor is the crux of the development (all the more since it is the one theme to change in character, and, in most performances, tempo, from its original form). This theme's tonic is B♭ in the ritornello and F in the exposition, then B♮ in the development and F♯ in the recapitulation, and D in the coda – which is to say that its first two tonics are the sixth and third degrees, respectively, of D minor (apart from their modes, which "must" be minor as already discussed) and its next two are those of D major (in the "right" modes automatically). If the movement's second half does gravitate toward D major in this sense, gradually preparing what will become explicit only in the latter part of the recapitulation, then the sense of the movement's form as a tripartite "sonata-allegro," exposition-development-recapitulation, with "introductory" ritornello, must be qualified by another: a pair of pairs, ritornello-exposition and development-recapitulation, with ritornello and development corresponding exactly in thematic sequence (and exposition and recapitulation adding the same material that is not in ritornello and development, although not otherwise matching entirely).[17]

There remains a great deal to say about the development, since the imagined descending chromatic line from which B♭'s absence is such an issue is only a crude representation of what actually happens. The most difficult passage is between C♮ and B♮: to identify these with the second and third themes (i.e., m. 259 and m. 278 or m. 287) takes a bit of work, and leaves a strong B♮ before the first C♮ (m. 244) and a strong C♮ after the last B♮ (m. 291). Many lines of motivic reference converge here, notably to the exposition's descent to C♮ and the recapitulation's "domesticating" attachment of C♮ to B♮, but the exact tracing of them is too long a job for this essay.

All that I will attempt is what seems most urgent, the identification of one last way to resolve the abnorm of succession – namely to "undo" it, C♮–C♯. This is one way to interpret the action over the long A pedal (especially recognizing its onset *as* a pedal in m. 297, not m. 295): as turning A-minor triads into potentially cadential A-major ones, and the turn from B♮ (m. 287) to C♮ (m. 291) can be assimilated to this. More remarkably, the entire succession D–C♯–C♮ is reversed in the elaboration of C♮ beginning in m. 259. The theme's usual change of mode comes with the succession C♮–C♯ (the latter in m. 263); and C♯, rewritten as D♭, starts a repetition one semitone higher, leading back to D♮ – or C𝄪 (m. 271). The soloist's contribution to this ascending sequence is a mind-boggling cross-reference to the B♭ abnorm, taking advantage of

17. Another interpretation of these key relations should be added: the first and fourth, B♭ minor and F♯ minor, are complementary about the movement's tonic of D minor, as are the second and third, F minor and B minor. For illustrations of such thinking in tonal contexts, see sec. 2, "Tonal Background," of David Lewin's "Inversional Balance as an Organizing Force in Schoenberg's Music and Thought" (*Perspectives of New Music* 6, no. 2 [Spring–Summer 1968]: 1–21).

the bass notes C♯ and D. When the low strings reach C♯ (m. 263), the piano seizes on the A-major six-three as delaying a C♯-minor five-three – which is to say, it interprets this chord as analogous to the abnormal B♭ six-three delaying the tonic. The piano's C♯-minor version of the theme runs its course to the major-mode E♯ (or F♮) over the low strings' second start of the tune in m. 267;[18] when the strings reach D♮ (or C×) in m. 271, the result is *exactly* the initial six-three (or its enharmonic equivalent). Recognizing this, the piano responds (in mm. 271–72) by changing its tune so that it will *not* resolve B♭ to A: its retention of B♭ once more preserves the abnormal chord from an implied resolution.[19] It is at the tune's original transposition that this reference is made (its F–C♭–B♭ contrasts the F–B♭–A of mm. 26–28); and, as though to suggest that recovering the abnorm substitutes for returning to the tonic, this ends the theme's story: it is omitted from the recapitulation.

In the coda, the abnormal succession runs in both directions – in its original direction as a linear succession early on and in its reversed direction within an idiosyncratically evolved harmonic progression virtually at the end. The final strategy of resolution integrates these two pitch classes with the pitch class B♭ (no longer B♮) in reference to D minor's subdominant, the context that can absorb them with least damage to D minor. When the orchestra rouses itself to join the piano in mm. 451–53, it combines a D-major triad, arpeggiated with the opening motive, and an upper line D–C♯–C♮ – the combination of C♯ with elements of the D-major triad producing a transitory F♯-minor triad (m. 452) on the way, one last time, into the F♯ diminished-seventh chord containing C♮. After all its history of deflections, this harmony at last resolves to what it has always implied, namely the subdominant of D minor, in m. 456. As well as the least disruptive outcome possible for C♯–C♮, this resolution establishes the least disruptive context possible for B♭. In the general context of approaching the dominant in m. 461, mm. 456–58 can then be understood to provide three different triadic "substitutes" for the abnormal B♭ chord, in rotation: the G-minor triad,

18. In mm. 267–68, the piano begins in C♯ (D♭) major as the low strings finish in A♯ (B♭) minor; the inner-voice G♯–G×–A♯ (A♭–A♮–B♭) that negotiates between these keys is barely recoverable as an allusion to the opening harmony – if the thread can be held until the low strings rise by their next semitone to C× (D) in m. 271.

19. The neighboring C♭ confers on the B♭ chord the remotest harmonic identity that it can sustain, that of an applied dominant to an E♭-minor (D♯) triad that never occurs, in the midst of a tricky modulation from B♭ (A♯) minor to C♭ (B♮) minor.

presenting B♭ "safely" after D–C♯–C♮; the E-major triad, which defused
the B♭ chord at the beginning of the recapitulation; and the D-minor
triad, for which the B♭ chord always was a substitute in the first place.

The dominant is yet again infiltrated by B♭, whose persistence prevents a resolution in m. 464 – but not by producing a B♭ triad: rather, the
harmonic framework is again that of the subdominant (here expansive
enough to absorb a passing B♭ triad at the end of m. 465). The subdominant coloration eventuates in the "traditional" Neapolitan approach to
the dominant (also readily available, but never reached, in the context
of B♭) in m. 469, but motivic particulars return: the dominant's C♯
is immediately approached, quite untraditionally, through the enharmonic equivalent of C♮. One final time, the tonic is inflected as the
dominant of the subdominant, to force one more approach to the cadence (in m. 470, with high E♭ recalling the context of the very first
abnormal C♮ in m. 21). This time, the approach to the cadence reaches
further into the key of the subdominant, drawing on its own subdominant as a replacement for the Neapolitan in m. 473, and thus creating a
harmonic progression marked by the atypical presence of C♮ in the pre-
dominant chord. After this, D minor is expansive and pointedly straightforward, expanded only by transitory references to the scales of its
subdominant and dominant (with raised sixth and seventh degrees).

* * *

Nonetheless, the issues raised in the first movement do not end here. In
a short space, it is possible to say only a few things about their persistence. The necessary framework is provided not so much by the abnorms themselves as by the contrast between D minor and D major
developed in the recapitulation, particularly as identified with the contrast between F and B♭, on one hand, and F♯ and B♮, on the other, as
secondary tonics. This becomes the contrast between the second and
third movements: in the second movement's ("peaceful") D major, F♯
minor (mm. 44ff.) and B♮ minor and major (mm. 52ff.) are the most
important subordinate keys, and in the third movement's ("stormy") D
minor, F major (mm. 42ff. and 275ff.) and B♭ major and minor (mm.
181ff.). The last movement's episode in B♭ is especially interesting for
its filling of the gap between D minor and B♭ minor, opened in the first
movement's ritornello: the theme's initial figure (mm. 181–82) alludes
to the first movement's opening figure in arpeggiating the B♭-major
triad through the same range, a tenth from D to F (see ex. 3.4); for the

Example 3.4: Correspondence of range between first movement's
opening melody and third movement's B♭-major melody.

first time in the concerto this triad is a tonic – the very tonic whose
omission is such an issue in the ritornello – and the fugue (beginning in
m. 238) makes the last connection by changing the mode to B♭ minor.[20]

This leaves C♯–C♮ to consider. Again the second movement contrasts
the first, by including C♮ as a prominent motivic element (in more
places than it would make sense to cite) while avoiding the *succession* C♯–
C♮ almost entirely.[21] The finale makes nothing much of C♮ in any context – until an animated dominant in mm. 360 ff. is deflected by C♮ in
the bass in m. 369, leading to a cadenza that includes the chromatic descent C♯–C♮ within the dominant (mm. 384ff.), much as the approach
to the first movement's recapitulation does. The outcome (in mm.
410–41) is a D-major version of the B♭-major theme (that is, of all that
remains of the B♭ abnorm) whose tonic triad is almost constantly inflected toward its subdominant by C♮. The subdominant in question is
now major, of course, and its arrival will resolve C♯–C♮ as completely as it
can be resolved, while decisively expunging B♭ and canonizing B♮. Strikingly, it does not occur within this passage, and neither occurs nor is
referred to within the *meno mosso* of mm. 442–62. It finally occurs during the *più animato* (mm. 463ff.), but is not established before the
passage passes through to *its* subdominant – that is, a C♮-major triad – in

20. This adds a sidelight to the relation between this finale and that of Beethoven's Piano
Concerto in C Minor, op. 37, demonstrated by Charles Rosen in "Influence: Plagiarism and
Inspiration" (*19th-Century Music* 4 [1980]: 91–93). Among many other parallels, Rosen
points out that in both finales "a staccato fugue . . . (m. 230 in Beethoven, m. 238 in
Brahms)" is followed by "the first appearance of the main theme in the major mode . . .
formed with a drone bass in pastoral style [m. 265 in Beethoven, m. 275 in Brahms]." As
Tovey observes (*Essays*, 3:74–75), the remarkable key of Beethoven's "pastoral" passage,
E major (identified most remarkably by Rosen as "the flat mediant major"), refers to the key
of the second movement; in Brahms's finale, analogous reference to a still unassimilated
remote key is made by the fugue.

21. A glorious exception is at the point of recapitulation (m. 58) – where, as a bonus, the root
relation F♯–D complements B♭–D.

m. 487. At this point, the most amazing thing happens (amazing even by the prevailing standards): a wild succession of major triads, C♮–A–F♮– D (in mm. 487, 491, 493, and 495) whose first move forcefully replaces C♮ with C♯ and whose second move as forcefully replaces C♯ with C♮. After this, the D-major triad again sounds like the dominant of its subdominant, the G–D alternation of mm. 497–98 delivers the tonicized subdominant that is the concerto's final response to C♮, and unproblematically affirmative dominants and tonics close the piece.

By the time all this is worked out, the abnorms have more than found their places in the system of D minor and major. Although I have consistently described the tonal norms with which the abnorms conflict as "larger," I would finally be unhappy to represent the abnorms' resolution as their yielding to the global norms' superior force. With justification I can say that the conflict ceases to be evident; what the abnorms motivate is no longer so different from what the norms allow. But this can be read as integration rather than overcoming – at least in the D-Minor Concerto.

Whichever way this process is interpreted, it should be recognized as characteristically Brahmsian in the prodigious depth of insight and energy of invention exerted to keep the tonality together. To a few of Brahms's contemporaries, and more than a few of his successors, the magnitude of forces on both sides – the power expended in resolution indicating the power of what must be resolved – could suggest another path as well: for there might be enough life in abnorms to sustain them on their own. The extent to which this life requires unequal conflict as the medium for its manifestation is debatable: perhaps the observable mutual independence of various norms, none elevated above the others by its standing in a literature or system, would suffice. The issue, indeed, has its own life – as a continuing fact of life for any of us who would be *gelernte Brahmsianer.*[22]

22. Paul Dessau, ". . . a few remarks Schoenberg made to me . . . ," *Perspectives of New Music* 11, no. 2 (Spring–Summer 1973): 84.

FOUR

From "Concertante Rondo" to "Lyric Sonata": A Commentary on Brahms's Reception of Mozart

John Daverio

I

Arnold Schoenberg's essay "Brahms the Progressive" (1947) is rich in musical examples. Just under half (twenty-five) come from the works of Brahms himself. But it is noteworthy that second place goes not to Beethoven, Wagner, Mahler, or Strauss, represented by about three examples apiece, but to Mozart, who is allotted eight. One might argue that the essay concerns Mozart as much as it does Brahms. Indeed, Schoenberg returns to Mozart again and again as the composer who, next to Brahms, moved farthest in the direction of an "unrestricted musical language." A portion of the first movement of Mozart's D-Minor String Quartet, K. 421, is held up as a model of "musical prose," Schoenberg's term of approbation for a concise presentation of musical ideas devoid of empty filler and simpleminded repetition. Similarly, the constructive technique that Schoenberg discerns in the third section of the act 2 Finale of *Le Nozze di Figaro* ("Susanna, son morta") – where the whole of the ensemble's musical fabric is determined by the reordering and variation of five apparently discontinuous musical segments – is judged nothing less than a "vision of the

I would like to thank Karol Berger and Laurence Dreyfus for their invitation to participate in the colloquium at Stanford University in May 1991 at which a shorter version of this essay was given, and David Rosen, Joseph Kerman, and Kofi Agawu for their insightful comments. Joel Galand (Yale University) also read an earlier draft of this essay; I thank him for calling my attention to a number of compositions that I might otherwise have missed.

future." In Schoenberg's estimation, we can find a comparable degree of independence from formal symmetry only in the music of Brahms.[1] This may strike us as an odd pairing: Mozart and Brahms. Then too, Schoenberg's tone is often strident, his intent polemical, his mode of argument tendentious. Yet might not a measure of critical truth be teased out of a view that pairs Mozart and Brahms – as progressives?

It has become a commonplace to assert that the richness of Brahms's music derives in large part from the richness of the tradition that it embodies and transcends. As Charles Rosen puts it, "With Brahms, we reach a composer whose music we cannot fully appreciate without becoming aware of the influences which went into its making."[2] Likewise, our sense for the Mozartean, Viennese Classical component of that tradition can only be enriched by charting the course of its reception in the nineteenth century. My aims here, therefore, are, first, to suggest that Mozart furnished the principal impetus for some of Brahms's most unusual essays in sonata style, works that, given their singular blending of rondo, sonata-allegro, concerto, and song-form elements, appear to stand somewhat apart from the Classical canon of forms and genres; and, second, to trace Brahms's transformation of the Mozartean design and thereby show how it was made to answer to the differing compositional concerns of distinct musical epochs.

While much has been written concerning Brahms's debt to Beethoven and Schubert,[3] little attention has been paid to his relationship with the music of Mozart. To be sure, Imogen Fellinger has recently summarized the biographical aspects of Brahms's lifelong preoccupation with Mozart: which of Mozart's works he knew and when and how he came into contact with them; his high regard for the piano sonatas and concertos, string quartets, late symphonies, and the Da Ponte operas; his avid collecting of Mozart's manuscripts; his involvement in the early

1. Arnold Schoenberg, "Brahms the Progressive," in *Style and Idea*, ed. Leonard Stein (Berkeley and Los Angeles: University of California Press, 1984), 398–441; see also Hermann Danuser, *Musikalische Prosa* (Regensburg: G. Bosse Verlag, 1975), 130.

2. Charles Rosen, "Influence: Plagiarism and Inspiration," *19th-Century Music* 4 (1980): 94.

3. Among many studies, see Musgrave, 118–28, 130–34, 224–28; Rosen, "Influence," 24–37, and his *Sonata Forms* (New York: W. W. Norton & Co., 1980), 322; Tovey, "Brahms's Chamber Music," in *Main Stream*, 244; James Webster, "Schubert's Sonata Form and Brahms's First Maturity," *19th-Century Music* 2 (1978): 18–35, and 3 (1979): 52–71; Robert Pascall, "Brahms and Schubert," *Musical Times* 124 (1983): 286–91; and Christopher Wintle, "The 'Sceptred Pall': Brahms's Progressive Harmony," in *Brahms* 2, 197–222.

phases of Mozart research, particularly as editor of the *Requiem*, K. 626, for the Breitkopf and Härtel *Gesamtausgabe*; and his careful study of Otto Jahn's biography and Köchel's *Verzeichnis*.[4] But modern criticism, as represented by Bernard Jacobson's remark that "Mozart's influence is less often [than that of Bach, Handel, Haydn, Beethoven, Schubert, or Schumann] to be found affecting Brahms in any explicit way," has scarcely recognized a *musical* relationship between the two.[5] It is probably fair to say that the Mozart-Brahms connection has been neglected because, for most commentators, Mozart's music adheres to an aesthetic of the Beautiful that is at odds with the nineteenth century's attunement to the Characteristic. For Carl Dahlhaus, whose stance on this point is representative, Mozart's approach to musical design can be compared to architecture, in that it is "the principle of balance which dominates and controls his forms of whatever order, from the subordinate clause to the overall outline of the whole."[6] Appraisals of this sort are themselves rooted in the mid- to late nineteenth-century tendency to idealize Mozart as the "Raphael of Music," the perfector of form, to view him as a composer who, apart from the demoniac overtones of *Don Giovanni* and the *Volkstümlichkeit* of *Die Zauberflöte*, offered little that was directly in line with the Romantic spirit.[7] Hanslick's equation of the essence of Mozart's music with its embodiment of the qualities of symmetry and restraint (*Maßhalt*) is still a part of our critical consciousness.[8] Thus, linking Mozart and Brahms might threaten to expose the latter to charges of epigonism that a half century of criticism has attempted to redress.

Brahms's departure from the norm in his own view of Mozart is therefore more than a little surprising. To be sure, he repeated the "perfection" topos that was common enough in his day: "Every number in

4. Imogen Fellinger, "Brahms's View of Mozart," in *Brahms*, 41–57.

5. Bernard Jacobson, *The Music of Brahms* (London: Tantivy Press, 1977), 34.

6. Carl Dahlhaus, "Issues in Composition," in *Between Romanticism and Modernism: Four Studies in the Music of the Later Nineteenth Century*, trans. Mary Whittall (Berkeley and Los Angeles: University of California Press, 1980), 50. See also Dahlhaus's *Die Musik des 18. Jahrhunderts: Neues Handbuch der Musikwissenschaft*, vol. 5 (Laaber: Laaber Verlag, 1985), 48.

7. See Karl Gustav Fellerer, "Mozart in der Musik des 19. Jahrhunderts," *Mozart Jahrbuch* (1980–83), 2–5.

8. Eduard Hanslick, *Concerte, Componisten und Virtuosen der letzten fünfzehn Jahre, 1870–1885* (Berlin: Allgemeiner Verein für deutschen Literatur, 1886), 62, 348.

Table 4.1. Mozart's Amplified Binary Movements

Date	Composition	Movement	Comments[a]
1775	K. 284, Piano Sonata in D	second (Rondeau en Polonaise)	1b
1776	K. 254, Divertimento in B♭	last (Rondeau)	1b
1777	K. 309, Piano Sonata in C	last (Rondeau)	1a, 1b, 3
1778	K. 314, Flute Concerto in D	last (Rondeau)	2, 3
	K. 299, Concerto for Flute and Harp in C	last (Rondeau)	1b, 2, 3
	K. 296, Sonata for Piano and Violin in C	last (Rondeau)	1b
	K. 306, Sonata for Piano and Violin in D	last	2, 3
1779	K. 364, *Sinfonia Concertante* for Violin and Viola in E♭	last	2, 3
1781	K. 375, Serenade for Winds in E♭	last (Finale)	1b
	K. 376, Sonata for Piano and Violin in F	last (Rondeau)	1b, 3
	K. 448, Sonata for Two Pianos in D	last	1b, 2
1782	K. 413, Piano Concerto in F	last	1b, 2, 3
	K. 414, Piano Concerto in A	last (Rondeau)	1b, 3
	K. 415, Piano Concerto in C	last (Rondeau)	1a, 3
1784	K. 456, Piano Concerto in B♭	last	1b, 3
	K. 459, Piano Concerto in F	last	2, 3
	K. 428, String Quartet in E♭	last	2
	K. 452, Quintet for Piano and Winds in E♭	last	1b, 3
	K. 457, Piano Sonata in C Minor	last	1b, 3
1785	K. 466, Piano Concerto in D Minor	last	2, 3
	K. 478, Piano Quartet in G Minor	last (Rondo)	1a, 1b, 3
1786	K. 488, Piano Concerto in A	last	1b, 3
	K. 493, Piano Quartet in E♭	last	1a, 1b, 3
1787	K. 526, Sonata for Piano and Violin in A	last	1a, 1b, 2, 3
	K. 515, String Quintet in C	last	1a
	K. 516, String Quintet in G Minor	last	1b, 2, 3
1788	K. 537, Piano Concerto in D	last	2, 3
	K. 563, Divertimento for String Trio in E♭	last	1a
	K. 542, Piano Trio in E	last	1a, 1b
	K. 548, Piano Trio in C	last	1b
1789	K. 575, String Quartet in D	last	1a
	K. 576, Piano Sonata in D	last	1a
1791	K. 595, Piano Concerto in B♭	last	2, 3
	K. 617, Adagio and Rondo for Harmonica, Flute, Oboe, Viola, and Cello	(Rondeau)	1a, 1b
	K. 622, Clarinet Concerto	last (Rondo)	1a, 1b, 2

a. 1a = developmental interruption; 1b = episodic interruption; 2 = conflation; 3 = scattering.

Mozart's *Figaro* is a miracle to me. It is absolutely unintelligible to me how anyone can create something so absolutely perfect. Never has it been done so again, not even by Beethoven."[9] But then too there is his ironic rejoinder to Richard Heuberger's assertion that, when compared with Mozart and Haydn, Beethoven was often less daring in his handling of form: "It's a good thing . . . that most people don't know that."[10] Indeed, the Mozartean form that seems to have had a special appeal for Brahms has little of the "Beautiful" about it. I am thinking primarily of the design that obtains in the thirty-odd movements drawn from Mozart's chamber and orchestral music listed in table 4.1 and that informs the group of Brahms movements in table 4.2. Each case is characterized by the following sequence of events: (1) a more or less conventional sonata-form exposition featuring two distinct theme groups and key areas; (2) an immediate return to the tonic (much as in a rondo) and the recurrence of a part of the opening theme group; (3) an amplification, either developmental, episodic, or both, of material from the first group and/or transition; (4) a recapitulation of the second group in the tonic; and (5) either an extended coda on the material of the opening or a more exact restatement of that material in the tonic. The design therefore is essentially bipartite. The first half sets forth the tonal and thematic argument of a sonata-form exposition; the second (responsive) portion serves as an amplification and tonal resolution of the first. Accordingly, the background model that Mozart enlarges is the simple period, a statement with modified repetition.

The Mozartean design, which did not figure in the accounts of the principal eighteenth- and nineteenth-century theorists (Koch, Kollmann, Reicha, Czerny, A. B. Marx, Dommer), has often been described by more recent commentators as a special variety of rondo; Mozart, after all, affixed the designation *Rondeau* to about half the movements listed in table 4.1. Yet there is some disagreement as to exactly *how* the design conforms to the rondo idea. The A B A C B′ A letter scheme usually linked to the form suggests a kind of sonata-rondo with the refrain statement between C and B′ omitted.[11] But, since in most cases Mozart

9. *Brahms und Billroth*, 315. (Unless otherwise noted, all translations are mine.) See also the similar remarks in Richard Heuberger, *Erinnerungen an Johannes Brahms: Tagebuchnotizen aus den Jahren 1885–1897*, ed. Kurt Hofmann (Tutzing: Hans Schneider, 1970), 12; and Kalbeck, *Brahms*, 2:171.

10. Heuberger, *Erinnerungen*, 22.

11. See Malcolm S. Cole, "The Development of the Instrumental Rondo Finale from 1750 to

Table 4.2. Brahms's Amplified Binary Movements

Date	Composition	Movement	Comments[a]
1857–58	Op. 11, Serenade No. 1 in D	sixth (Rondo)	1a
1861	Op. 25, Piano Quartet in G Minor	first	1a
		fourth (*Rondo alla Zingarese*)	1b, 3
1861–62	Op. 26, Piano Quartet in A	fourth	2
1861–64	Op. 34, Piano Quintet in F Minor	fourth	2
1865–73	Op. 51, no. 1, String Quartet in C Minor	fourth	2
1855–76	Op. 68, Symphony No. 1 in C Minor	fourth	2
1878	Op. 77, Violin Concerto in D	third	1b, 3
1880–81	Op. 81, *Tragic* Overture		1a, 1b
1878–81	Op. 83, Piano Concerto No. 2 in B♭	fourth	1a
1883	Op. 90, Symphony No. 3 in F	fourth	2
1884–85	Op. 98, Symphony No. 4 in E Minor	second	2, 3
		third	1a
1886	Op. 101, Piano Trio in C Minor	first	1a, 1b, 2, 3
1886–88	Op. 108, Sonata for Violin and Piano in D Minor	fourth	1a
1889	Op. 8, Piano Trio in B (2nd version)	fourth	2
1890	Op. 111, String Quintet in G	fourth	1a
1891	Op. 114, Clarinet Trio in A Minor	fourth	2
1892	Op. 116, no. 1, Capriccio		1a
1894	Op. 120, no. 1, Sonata for Clarinet and Piano in F Minor	fourth	1a, 1b

a. 1a = developmental interruption; 1b = episodic interruption; 2 = conflation; 3 = scattering.

closes C with a reworking of the transitional material that earlier had led to the second group (B), it seems misleading to speak of an "omission" here: when B′ follows this transitional passage, we do in fact hear what we have been led to expect. Thus Rosen's interpretation of the finales of the C-Major Piano Sonata, K. 309, and the G-Minor String Quartet,

1800," 2 vols. (Ph.D. diss., Princeton University, 1964), 1:110–18, 189–90, 212, 215, 219, and "Rondo," in *The New Grove Dictionary of Music and Musicians*, ed. Stanley Sadie (London: Macmillan, 1980), 16:175.

K. 516, as sonata-rondos with reverse recapitulations (A+B A C B'+A) confuses matters; it obscures the fact that B' proceeds smoothly and logically out of C and that these two form parts constitute a coherent syntactic unit, one standing apart from the closing A, which acts rather more like a coda than a recapitulation.[12]

By the same token, the Brahms movements listed in table 4.2 have not been considered as a group because of differences of opinion over their status as sonata forms or rondos.[13] Tovey, for example, described the Finale of the D-Minor Violin Sonata, op. 108, as "a powerful sonata rondo with a grandly tragic climax" and the Finale of the Clarinet Trio, op. 114, as containing "everything that a full-sized sonata movement has room for"; but for Robert Pascall both are sonata forms, and for Michael Musgrave they are rondos.[14] These discrepancies suggest that coming down in favor of one or another form type (or letter scheme) is less useful than recognizing Mozart's and Brahms's play on the same set of formal ambiguities.[15] If the textbook sonata-rondo (A B A C A B A) is itself an equivocal blend of form types, the Mozart/Brahms sonata(?)-rondo(?) compounds the ambiguity, and the interpretive differences that I have noted merely serve to point up the duality of the form.

But, if pressed to affix a name to our design, I would opt for *amplified binary*, an admittedly neutral and colorless term, but at least an accurate one. Here I am following the lead of Tovey, who noted that the Finale of Brahms's F-Minor Piano Quintet, op. 34, is "a big binary movement with the development section omitted, or rather replaced by a considerable discussion between the recapitulation of the 'first subject' and that of the second."[16] Tovey was essentially correct in observing that this

12. Rosen, *Sonata Forms*, 121–25.

13. For a discussion of opp. 25/i, 26/iv, 34/iv, 51, no. 1/iv, 68/iv, 90/iv, 98/ii, 98/iii, 101/i, 108/iv, 8/iv (second version), and 114/iv as unusual sonata-form variants, see Robert Pascall, "Some Special Uses of Sonata Form by Brahms," *Soundings* 4 (1974): 58–63. See also Musgrave, 96–100 (on op. 25/i), 101 (op. 26/iv), 105 (op. 34/iv), 113 (op. 51, no. 1/iv), 134 (op. 68/iv), and 197 (op. 101/i).

14. Tovey, "Brahms's Chamber Music," 264, 266; Pascall, "Special Uses," 58; and Musgrave, 192, 251.

15. Readings biased toward one form type, and one alone, often tend to be forced. Robert Bailey, for instance, treats op. 90/iv as a sonata-form movement with the first group omitted from the recapitulation and displaced into the coda (see "Musical Language and Structure in the Third Symphony," in *Brahms Studies*, 412–15).

16. Tovey, "Brahms's Chamber Music," 244.

form was passed on to Brahms from Mozart by way of Schubert, but, as is so often the case, the illuminating remark is lacking elaboration.[17] We might surmise that the Schubert movements that Tovey had in mind are the finales of the String Quartet in A Minor, D. 804, the String Quartet in G, D. 887, the String Quintet in C, D. 956, and the Piano Sonata in B♭, D. 960, all of which approach the amplified binary design. We might note in addition several similar instances in Beethoven's output: the slow movement of the D-Major String Quartet, op. 18, no. 3, and the finales of the E-Minor "Razumovsky" Quartet, op. 59, no. 2, the Fourth Piano Concerto, op. 58, and the F-Minor "Serioso" Quartet, op. 95. Still, the Mozartean precedents seem more relevant. Not only did Mozart offer Brahms a greater number of models to reinterpret,[18] but both Mozart and Brahms also employed remarkably similar structural devices that bypass Beethoven and Schubert altogether.

Brahms left next to nothing in the way of verbal criticism on music. His criticism is rather to be found in his compositions themselves, especially those – like the works under consideration here – that draw on much earlier models. For Mozart, the amplified binary was most often associated with the final movements of concertos or concertante chamber music and thus can be understood as a kind of concerto form that mediated between the easygoing character that late eighteenth-century etiquette demanded of finales and the weightier, more serious conceits expected of opening movements. The Mozartean amplified binary is, in effect, a concertante rondo. For Brahms, the situation is drawn differently. Although he too associated the design with the concerto or with chamber music involving piano, he also employed it regularly in purely symphonic works. Not only did he imbue the concerto with symphonic traits, but, in works like the Tragic Overture, op. 81 (where the protracted recurrence of material from the opening group is reserved for the closing passages, much as in a concerto ritornello), he did the

17. Tovey's remarks have occasioned a few glosses. For instance, Musgrave (p. 105) suggests the Finale of Schubert's C-Major String Quintet as a model for the op. 34 Finale; likewise, Pascall mentions the last movement of Mozart's D-Major Piano Sonata, K. 576 (one of thirty-some cases!), as a possible model for Brahms's unusual sonata-form movements ("Special Uses," 63).

18. Although we can safely assume Brahms's familiarity with most of the Mozart movements listed in table 4.1, specific connections are more readily made in some cases than in others (see the appendix to this essay).

reverse.[19] More important, the Mozartean design afforded Brahms a means of organizing and presenting musical material whose lyric expansiveness was inimical to the tightly knit, dynamic arguments of sonata style. Brahms's purely musical critique of Mozart spanned practically the entire length of his creative career – from the early Serenade in D, op. 11, the first of his classicizing symphonic compositions, through the chamber music with piano conceived during the period of his "first maturity" and the symphonic masterpieces of the 1870s and 1880s, to the enigmatic, aphoristic works of his last years. At the heart of the critique was a transformation of concertante rondo into lyric sonata.

II

In addition to the general traits of the Mozart/Brahms amplified binary described above, we should consider four additional procedures that often characterize the form. In some cases, the orderly recurrence of first group and transitional material in the second half of the design is interrupted by a developmental or episodic passage that, when the form is considered as a whole, creates a "bulge" in the first phase of the responsive portion – an expansion in the most literal sense. Application of the second procedure may likewise result in an expansion, although here there is no interruption, no bulge. It can be described as a fusion or "conflation" of recapitulatory and developmental processes,[20] involving the reappearance of first group and transitional material in a corresponding position in the response, where it is subjected to motivic and tonal elaboration; most frequently, the opening of the first group recurs in the tonic, while the remainder is thematically and tonally developed. Both procedures affect the place in sonata-style works that historically has been a potential area for developmental expansion: the sensitive interface between first and second groups in the recapitulation, where the tonal digression of the exposition must be counterbalanced by main-

19. See also the commentary in James Webster, "Brahms's Tragic Overture: The Form of Tragedy," in *Brahms*, 110. The Academic Festival Overture, op. 80, a kind of humorous complement to op. 81 and by far the least discussed of Brahms's major orchestral works, shares some traits with the compositions discussed in this essay. The special issues that it raises, however – in particular, Brahms's adaptation of the potpourri or quodlibet principle – merit separate consideration.

20. I borrow the term from Pascall, who has applied it to many of Brahms's sonata-form movements (see "Special Uses," 58).

taining, or steering, the tonal course toward the tonic.[21] What marks Mozart's and Brahms's handling of these two procedures – and helps firm the connection between them – is that, while Beethoven and Schubert tend to employ each separately, Brahms and Mozart often *combine* them within a single piece (see the far right column in tables 4.1 and 4.2).[22]

The third procedure, whereby material from the first group is redistributed or "scattered" throughout the responsive portion of the design, similarly is limited to the works of Mozart and Brahms, albeit handled somewhat differently by the two. Finally, Mozart and Brahms often adopt a similar line in casting the coda, the form part that, as Joseph Kerman has noted, is too often overlooked by analysts.[23] Although we are likely to think of Beethoven as the composer who most thoroughly enriched the closing paragraphs of his sonata-style works (and, indeed, there is much of Beethoven in Brahms's codas), many of Mozart's amplified binary movements feature terminal references to the whole of the principal material that has come before.[24] The condensed reprise, or *summarizing coda*, as I will call it, likewise figures in Brahms's conception of the design, often serving to highlight, at the formal level, the lyric quality that pervades his thematic material. *Can-*

21. See Rosen, *Sonata Forms*, 250.

22. In some works, like the opening movement of Brahms's C-Minor Piano Trio, op. 101, or the finales of Mozart's A-Major Piano and Violin Sonata, K. 526, and G-Minor String Quintet, K. 516, the various procedures – episodic *and* developmental expansion, developmental/recapitulatory fusion – are blended so artfully that it becomes difficult to distinguish them.

23. See Joseph Kerman, "Notes on Beethoven's Codas," in *Beethoven Studies 3*, ed. Alan Tyson (Cambridge: Cambridge University Press, 1982), 141.

24. Kerman points out (ibid., 149–51) that Beethoven often employed the coda as a field of resolution for some sort of thematic or tonal tension present in the first theme group, a device echoed in many of the Brahms movements considered here. Thus, the move to E♭ in the first group of op. 101 is recapitulated at the lower fifth (A♭) in the coda (mm. 199–201). Similarly, the D♭ (♭VI) chorale-like melody that figures in the opening group of the Finale of the Third Symphony, op. 90 (a recall of material from the second movement), is given a tonic restatement in the coda (mm. 280–96), just as the E♭ (♭III) tutti outburst in the first group of op. 98/iii (mm. 199–203) is presented in the tonic (C) during the closing paragraphs of the movement (mm. 337–41). While the thematic linking of first group and coda suggests the influence of Beethoven, the nature of the tonal relationships, involving the recurrence of material in ♭III or ♭VI either at the lower fifth or in the tonic, probably owes more to Schubert's preference for similar relationships in the expositions and recapitulations of his later sonata-style works.

tabile themes are thus complemented by a quasi-strophic overall design.

The following discussion will center on each of these four procedures in turn. In every instance, one or more of Brahms's movements is coupled with one or more of Mozart's. This is not meant to suggest either that we are dealing with instances of direct modeling or even that Mozart served as Brahms's only point of departure. My purpose rather is to emphasize the structural similarities that affirm a connection between the two composers and at the same time to register the distance that clearly separates them – a gap often mediated by the example of Beethoven and Schubert.

The Finale of the D-Minor Violin Sonata, op. 108, demonstrates the procedure of expansion through developmental interruption, as indicated in table 4.3, which aligns corresponding events in both halves of the design. The alignment has the advantage of showing that the entire stretch of music from m. 114 to m. 217 is in fact a recomposition of mm. 1–38 and that the first group and transition in the first half form a structural unit that is eventually subjected to elaborative expansion.[25] It is worth noting that tonal and thematic reprise are out of phase, a common enough occurrence in Brahms's music.[26] Measures 114–17 do double duty as thematic return and tonal retransition from the minor dominant (via its own dominant) to the tonic (via its subdominant). Although the music of mm. 134–93 may be described as a displacement of the development proper (and any graphic presentation of the form will make it appear so), it is quite logically tied to and spun out of the first theme group. Just as the opening theme consists of four successively varied and functionally differentiated statements of a four-measure idea (with the fourth statement being most obviously tied to the first),[27] so

---

25. Brahms adheres to a principle of Classical form that was codified by August Kollmann (among other theorists) in his *Essay on Practical Musical Composition* (London, 1799). For Kollmann, the first "section" (exposition) of a "long movement" consists of two subsections, the first containing "the setting out from the key towards its fifth in major, or third in minor" (i.e., the first group and transition) (see *Essay*, 5).

26. On this point, see Reinhold Brinkmann, "Anhand von Reprisen," in *Brahms-Analysen,* ed. Friedhelm Krummacher and Wolfram Steinbeck (Kassel: Bärenreiter, 1984), 107–20; Christian Martin Schmidt, *Johannes Brahms und seine Zeit* (Laaber: Laaber Verlag, 1983), 122–31; and Rosen, *Sonata Forms,* 322–24.

27. The second and third statements (mm. 5–7) constitute the theme proper; the off-tonic beginning of the first statement makes for an introductory gesture, while the half cadence of the fourth provides a link with the ensuing transition.

Table 4.3. Brahms, Sonata for Violin and Piano, Op. 108,
Fourth Movement (Presto agitato): Formal Plan

Part 1			Part 2		
Measure	*Description*	*Key*	*Measure*	*Description*	*Key*
1	First Group: a (4+4+4+4)	Dm	114	First Group: a	(V/Am– iv/Dm)– Dm
			134	Developmental Interruption: on a	Gm–B♭m– C♯m–Fm– (Gm)
			194	Recomposed Transition: b (references to a)	–V/Dm
17	Transition: b (references to a)	–V/Am			
39	Second Group	(C)–Am	218	Second Group	(F)–Dm
			293–	Coda:	Dm
			337	on a; closing refer- ences to b	

the developmental "bulge" continues to work out the same phrase, binding it to an ascending minor-third tonal chain: G minor–B♭ minor–C♯ minor. The expected move to E is expressively shifted up by a half step for a thunderous statement of the opening theme in F minor; from this point, the main tonal shifts proceed by fifth to A, the dominant, in preparation for the recomposed transition (mm. 194–217), which is likewise motivically linked to the first group. Both first group and developmental interruption, then, comprise four statements of the opening idea, which is first elaborated within a rhythmically symmetrical and tonally stable framework and then varied through more dynamic processes.

The Finale of Mozart's Piano Sonata in D, K. 576, presents a similar situation (see table 4.4): the developmental expansion is localized in much the same spot and likewise is limited to first-group material. That Mozart's first group is organized differently from Brahms's – as an antecedent/consequent period followed by a new idea that leads to a half cadence – does not gainsay the formal parallels. Like Brahms, Mozart plays on the expressive possibilities of third relationships in the respon-

Table 4.4. Mozart, Piano Sonata in D, K. 576, Third Movement
(Allegretto): Formal Plan

Part 1			Part 2		
Measure	*Description*	*Key*	*Measure*	*Description*	*Key*
	First Group:			First Group:	
1	a (?!)	D	65	a (?!)	D
17	b	–V/D	80	on b (terminally extended)	–V/F
				Developmental Interruption:	
			95	on a (sequential)	F–Gm
			103	on a (imitative)	A–Bm–V/D
	Transition:			Recomposed Transition:	
26	on a (sequential)	(A)–	117	on a (sequential)	D–
34	on a (imitative)	V/A–	125	on a (imitative)	V/D–
44	Second Group	A	135	Second Group	D
58	Retransition	–V/D	149	Retransition	–V/D
			163–	Coda:	D
			189	on a (?!)	

Note: ?! = antecedent, consequent.

sive part of the form, here by moving to ♭III (F). But Mozart's interruption takes as its organizational parallel, not the first group, as in Brahms, but the two elided phrases of the transition.[28] It proceeds in two phases: first, a sequential treatment of the opening gesture moving from F to G minor (mm. 95–102); second, a continuation of the sequential rise through A and B minor, with the opening gesture in close imitation (mm. 103–16). The two phases, then, exactly mirror the sequential and imitative components of the original transition to the dominant (mm.

28. What I am calling the transition does set out from the dominant, A major, although the latter is not affirmed as the new tonal area until m. 44, following on four measures of V/V prolongation.

26–33, 34–43) and its recomposed variant in the responsive half of the form (mm. 117–24, 125–34).

This kind of motivic limitation (and that in the developmental interludes in the finales of K. 515, K. 563, and K. 575) is sure to have impressed the motivically economical Brahms. But usually Mozart prefers episodic (i.e., melodically luxuriant) to developmental expansiveness; more often than not, the amplification in the second half of his design is due to the introduction of new material in the initiatory structural unit, now conceived as first group–episodic expansion–recomposed transition. Sometimes, as in the last movements of the C-Minor Piano Sonata, K. 457 (mm. 154–55), or the C-Major Piano and Violin Sonata, K. 296 (mm. 86–89), an episode makes fleeting reference to a motive from the first group, but such gestures tend to be less substantive than incidental to the main argument.

Brahms, whose departure from Mozart is often mediated by Beethovenian examples (toward the kind of thematic limitation that characterizes the developmental interlude in op. 59, no. 2/iv, mm. 142–93), presents us with the opposite situation. His expansive interludes (e.g., in op. 11/v, mm. 142–88; op. 25/i, mm. 171–236; op. 83/iv, mm. 173–251; and op. 116/i, mm. 67–131) are almost without exception tightly bound to material already presented, so that one must look long and hard for anything really "new." And Schubert's influence here would seem to be less than that of either Mozart or Beethoven. In the Finale of the C-Major String Quintet (where the developmental "bulge," mm. 214–66, is indeed limited to first-group music), Schubert makes do without any transitional material whatsoever, creating an obviously sectional effect that Brahms usually avoids.[29] What would have more readily attracted Brahms is the tonal plan of the quintet's development, which hinges on the disposition of two major-third pairs (C minor/E and B minor/E♭) expressively linked by a semitone shift.

29. The Finale of Schubert's Sonata in B♭, D. 960, is somewhat more complicated. Its sprawling, seventy-three-measure first group is itself organized as a rondo-like structure with a threefold statement of the opening theme. Since the developmental interruption comes between the first and the second appearances of the theme (mm. 265–322), the design, like that of the String Quintet Finale, maintains a sectional profile. Given its placement just after a more or less complete statement of the first group and its progress toward the very same music – and at the same tonal level – that had proceeded from the opening group in the first half of the form, the developmental interruption in the Finale of the A-Minor String Quartet, D. 804 (mm. 172–234) is in a sense syntactically "unnecessary"; Schubert's expansion is perceived as an insertion pure and simple, a truly "displaced" development.

Most telling for the Brahms/Mozart connection, however, are those instances where expansion results from the appearance of *both* episodic and developmental passages, a practice without precedent in Beethoven or Schubert. In the closing movements of Mozart's K. 478, K. 493, and K. 542, for instance, the "bulge" in the response results from the appearance of a new theme followed by development of earlier material. Brahms does much the same in the witty Finale of the Clarinet Sonata in F Minor, op. 120, no. 1, although he reverses Mozart's usual order of presentation within the "bulge": the response (mm. 77ff.) sets out with the main theme in the tonic and then proceeds to an elaborative reworking of this music (mm. 101–18) leading to a new tune in the relative minor (derived from the foregoing measures by means of Brahms's characteristic *Knüpftechnik*). In keeping with the Classicizing tone of the movement are Brahms's avoidance of ♭III relationships in favor of diatonic ones (the episode in the submediant recalling similar tonal arrangements in the finales of Mozart's K. 478, K. 493, and K. 542) and his subjection of the principal idea to straightforward variation on its recurrence (after the manner of Mozart's K. 575 finale). Thus, while Brahms may have derived his sense for motivic working out from Beethoven and his fondness for leisurely song themes and third relationships more clearly from Schubert, his exploitation of the structural possibilities of combinative forms stems largely from Mozart.

This "elective affinity" also manifests itself in those instances where Brahms fuses or conflates development and recapitulation, a procedure noted in almost half the movements in table 4.2. What is most striking for our purposes is the degree to which the design of a movement like the Finale of the String Quartet in C Minor, op. 51, no. 1, approximates that of, for example, Mozart's K. 428 (cf. tables 4.5 and 4.6). In both there is a direct correspondence between events in the responsive and expository portions of the form, with developmental reworking centered in the second presentation of the first group and transition, although Brahms begins to elaborate this material sooner than does Mozart. True, the two works are far removed from one another in character, tonal disposition, and motivic plan: Mozart retains the ethos, if not the conventional form, of a rondo; Brahms writes one of his most turbulent sonata-style essays. Mozart's tonal plan hinges on the polarity of tonic and dominant; Brahms's, on a complex web of third and Neapolitan relationships that allows the C minor/E♭ of the exposition to be answered by A minor/C in the responsive part of the

Table 4.5. Brahms, String Quartet in C Minor, Op. 51, No. 1,
Fourth Movement (Allegro); Formal Plan

Part 1			Part 2		
Measure	*Description*	*Key*	*Measure*	*Description*	*Key*
	First Group:			First Group:	
1	a (pseudo-?!; mm. 1–12, 13–21)[a]	(Cm)	94	on a!	Cm–
			102	on a	C#m–
			110	on a?	Am–
21	a′	Cm	120	on a′ (last 4 mm.)	
33	b	Cm– V/E♭	124	b	–V/C
41	Transition:		132	Recomposed Transition:	
	c (references to b and a)	V/E♭–		c (references to b and a)	V/C–
50	Second Group:	E♭	141	Second Group:	C
	references to c and a	(also Gm, Cm)		references to c and a	(also Em, Am)
			194	Coda:	Cm
				on a (?!) ex- tended (mm. 194–230) and b	

Note: ?! = antecedent, consequent.

form.[30] Mozart luxuriates in melodic abundance; Brahms infuses every form part with variants of the opening gesture. Yet the formal principles that govern the relationship of the parts are fundamentally the same. And again Brahms's approach to developmental/recapitulatory confla- tion comes closer to that of Mozart than to either Beethoven's or Schu- bert's. The extreme compression that Beethoven achieves in the last

30. For a complete discussion of this point, see Arnold Whittall, "Two of a Kind? Brahms's Op. 51 Finales," in *Brahms 2*, 150–57.

Table 4.6. Mozart, String Quartet in E♭, K. 428, Fourth Movement
(Allegro vivace): Formal Plan

Part 1			Part 2		
Measure	*Description*	*Key*	*Measure*	*Description*	*Key*
	First Group:			First Group:	
1	aba′	E♭	140	aba′	E♭
35	b		174	on b (extended)	E♭–Fm–V/Gm
	Transition:			Recomposed Transition:	
43	c	Cm–	186	on c (extended)	Gm–Fm–
54	d	V/B♭	201	d	V/E♭
60	Second Group	B♭	207	Second Group	E♭
131	Retransition	–V/E♭	278	Retransition	–V/E♭
			297–	Coda:	E♭
			342	on opening binary unit	

movement of the *Quartetto serioso*, for example, is almost without parallel
in Brahms. Conversely, the Finale of Schubert's G-Major String Quartet
is distinguished by a prolixity that is equally uncommon in Brahms: the
seventy measures of the first group grow to nearly two hundred in the
response.

Mozart frequently couples the conflation of development and recapitulation with the technique that I have called *scattering* (a device that
figures not at all in Beethoven and Schubert), whereby first-group music
is redistributed or reordered during the course of the responsive portion of the amplified binary form. For Mozart, scattering is a principle
more specifically associated with the opening movements of his concertos and is closely bound up with the layout of their expositions: a
series of ideas presented by the orchestra, followed by a series of ideas
presented by soloist and orchestra, some taken over from the opening
ritornello, some newly fashioned to dramatize the soloist's presence,
but in any event modulating to the dominant. The Mozartean recapitulation can be seen to provide not only tonal and melodic resolution
but *textural* resolution as well, for it features the interlacing of these
previously discontinuous ideas: the music of the opening orchestral

{127}

statement is literally "scattered" throughout the recapitulation. Thus a theme originally given out by the orchestra alone is often shared by orchestra and soloist in the recapitulation and thereby texturally "resolved."[31] When Mozart uses the technique in the concluding movement of a concerto or concertante chamber work, we may interpret it as a means of imbuing the traditionally lighthearted Classical finale with greater seriousness by bringing it more in line with the formal elaboration associated with opening movements.[32]

Let us consider the use of the scattering technique in the Finale of the D-Minor Piano Concerto, K. 466, a work that Brahms greatly admired. Its lengthy first group consists of (1) the principal theme, set off by a Mannheim rocket figure and growing into a periodic structure with a somewhat extended consequent phrase; (2) the orchestra's imitative reworking of the same, followed by two "thematic accessories" (Tovey), the first marked by a chromatic ascent and complementary descent, the second a cadential phrase; and (3) a new idea that dramatizes the reentry of the soloist (just as a new idea often marks the entrance of the soloist in the first movement of a concerto). In the responsive part of the form, this thematic complex is radically altered and rearranged (see table 4.7). Although the opening idea and its orchestral variant, both in the tonic, articulate the beginning of the response (mm. 167ff.), a variant of the first accessory does not recur until the *buffa* coda (mm. 370ff.), where it is significantly transformed in the major mode and shared by piano and orchestra. The second accessory recurs just after the recapitulation of the second group (mm. 337ff.), thus preparing for the cadenza, while the new idea linked with the soloist does not reappear at all in the tonic, serving instead as the main subject for the lengthy developmental discussion just before the tonic return of

31. Compare Tovey's characteristically insightful and concise remarks apropos of the principle of recapitulation in the first movements of Mozart's concertos: "The recapitulation in the tonic is a recapitulation of the opening tutti as well as of the first solo. It does not omit the features peculiar to the solo, but adds to them those features of the ritornello which the solo had not at first adopted. In particular, it is likely to follow the course of the opening much more closely than in the first solo; and the subsequent appearance of a previously neglected theme is the most conspicuous result of this tendency" (*Essays*, 3:23).

32. Tovey hints at this when he says that "the essential feature in the concerto finale is that the solo player states the theme, and the orchestra gives a counterstatement, to which it appends a long string of other themes, none of which is destined to reappear until the last stages of a work, where they all troop in and make a triumphant end" (ibid., 41).

Table 4.7. Mozart, Piano Concerto in D Minor, K. 466, Third Movement (Allegro assai): Redistribution of First-Group Material

Mm. 1–13, "rondo" theme (piano)	=	mm. 167–80 (piano)
13–29, imitative elaboration of the above (orchestra)	=	180–95 (orchestra)
30–50, first accessory (orchestra)	=	370–94 (piano + orchestra)
51–62, second accessory (orchestra)	=	337–45 (orchestra)
63–73, soloist's reentry theme	=	196–206, 230–70 (piano + orchestra)

the second group, thus highlighting the point where development and recapitulation are conflated. When the first group recurs, in other words, its elements undergo functional alterations, tonal and thematic development, and redistribution. All this of course allows Mozart to interweave – to resolve texturally – material first associated specifically with the piano or the orchestra. And just as Mozart here applies a first-movement technique to a finale, so he often transfers it from the concerto to his chamber music with piano, most clearly in the finales of K. 478, K. 493, and K. 526.

Brahms too makes use of the scattering technique in his concertos and chamber music for piano and strings, but with quite a different end in view. We can measure the departure from Mozart's usual practice in, for example, the Finale of the Violin Concerto, op. 77. In this movement there are no orchestral accessories: the first group is built entirely of varied presentations of the opening idea, an eight-measure phrase modulating from D to B minor, which is itself dominated by the motivic-rhythmic figure presented in the first measure. But the four phrases of the first group – the second an orchestral repetition of the first, the third moving from relative minor to tonic, and the fourth corresponding more nearly to the first but remaining in the tonic – are redistributed when they next appear. The response (mm. 93–221) begins with the first two phrases, while the second pair is withheld until just after the recapitulation of the second group (mm. 187–221), where they also prepare for the ensuing accompanied cadenza. The redistribution of material allows the first theme to act as a frame for the entire second part of the form, so that thematic scattering is put at the service of motivic cohesiveness. Indeed, the first theme not only frames the response but actually infiltrates it: even the G-major "episode" preceding the recapitulation of the second group (mm. 120–42) is shot through with references to the opening motive.

Nowhere does Brahms employ the technique more impressively as part of a larger process of motivic saturation than in the first movement of the C-Minor Piano Trio, op. 101 (see table 4.8). The first group is cast as a ternary unit, its third phrase drastically compressing the music of the first and opening out into the transition, its middle phrase providing thematic contrast by a move to E♭. These elements are extended like an ever-widening net over the remainder of the movement. Thus the move to E♭ in m. 12 (already presaged in m. 2) foreshadows the tonality of the second group, whose principal motive – a rising tetrachord – is prefigured in the opening measures of the movement. The three phrases of the first group are then redistributed throughout the responsive portion and coda (see the boxed-in areas in table 4.8): the recapitulation of the first phrase is divided between mm. 81–86 and mm. 134–39 (a developmental/episodic expansion of the first two phrases of the first group occupying the space between), and the recurrence of the second and third phrases (in the context of the tonic) is reserved for a threefold varied presentation in the coda, as if to compensate for their previous omission.[33] As in the Violin Concerto, scattering is employed as part of a process whereby the opening theme group is densely elaborated, both thematically and tonally. Also, it is used as a means of withholding closure until the last possible moment, so that greater formal weight is placed on the end of the movement.

It is not only the initial phase of the response that Mozart and Brahms subject to amplification but the concluding paragraphs as well. In several of the finales of Mozart's concertos (K. 364, K. 413, K. 466, K. 488, K. 622), concertante chamber works (K. 376, K. 563), and piano sonatas (K. 448, K. 457), the breadth of the coda results from a reworking of material from both the first and the second theme groups. The coda in the last movement of the C-Minor Piano Sonata, K. 457 (mm. 221–319), for instance, amounts to far more than a simple repetition of the opening tune, rondo fashion. Mozart begins by stating the opening group but proceeds to extend its closing flourishes, much as he had just before the episodic "bulge" (mm. 143–44) earlier on in the response.

33. For a reading of the form of this movement differing in some details from mine, see James Webster, "The General and the Particular in Brahms's Later Sonata Forms," in *Brahms Studies*, 72.

Table 4.8. Brahms, Piano Trio in C Minor, Op. 101, First Movement
(Allegro energico): Formal Plan

Part 1			Part 2		
Measure	*Description*	*Key*	*Measure*	*Description*	*Key*
	First Group:			First Group:	
1	a	Cm	81	on a (mm. 1–4)	Cm–
			91	on a	A♭–
			98	on a (episodic)	C♯m–
11	b	(E♭)–	113	on b (developmental)	A/F♯–B♭/G (= V/C)
			134	on a (mm. 5–11)	V/C
20	a′	Cm			
26	Transition	V/E♭	140	Recomposed Transition	V/C
38	Second Group	E♭	150	Second Group	C
				Coda:	
			193	on a (cf. mm. 81–82)	Cm
			199	b	(A♭)–
			208	on a′	Cm
			212	on b	
			216	on a′	
			220	on b	
			226	on a	

This leads logically enough to a variant of the earlier episode (cf. mm. 275–86 and mm. 146–66) and then to the real point of the passage: the recurrence of closing material from the exposition, last heard in mm. 90–96 in the relative major and not yet recapitulated in the tonic (mm. 287ff.). A terminal expansion of this sort in fact functions as a condensed recapitulation, a précis of all that has gone before, therefore placing the coda on a practically equal footing with the form parts preceding it.

The summarizing coda likewise figures in the finales of Brahms's opp. 11, 34, and 77, the closing paragraphs of which bring altered restatements of music from both first and second groups. Of course, the departure from Mozart is equally significant: Brahms is apt to alter rhythm and tempo (as in op. 77) or meter (op. 34), thus producing rather far-reaching thematic transformations. Of particular interest is the handling of second-group material in the coda of the Violin Concerto. When presented in the exposition (mm. 57–73), the second group hovers ambiguously between the dominant (A) and its dominant

{131}

(E); and the recapitulation of this music in mm. 150–66 is suspended with equal ambiguity between the subdominant (G) and D (heard in context as V/G). Only in the coda (mm. 292–304, 315–27) does it appear within a clearly tonic framework. And, inasmuch as Brahms alternates statements of first- and second-group music, the coda is imparted a self-contained rondo design of its own.

III

In the foregoing I have stressed the similarities between Mozart's and Brahms's approach to musical structure – and minimized the influence of Beethoven and Schubert on Brahms – first, in order to avoid creating the impression that we are dealing with the straightforward and logical evolution of an idealized pattern and, second, to establish that Brahms's was a Romanticizing gesture of appropriation, a reaching back into a distant past as a means of addressing musical concerns that he felt in all their presentness. In short, the amplified binary represents a "solution" to what were in essence quite different and historically specific problems. Insofar as it can be reconstructed from the comments of eighteenth- and nineteenth-century theorists, the horizon of expectations of Mozart's listeners demanded of the concerto finale a certain form (usually some variety of rondo), content (in the guise of virtuoso figuration), and style (manifested in the generally *buffa* character of the melodic material).[34] Mozart may be said to have "invented" the amplified binary (much as he probably created the first examples of the full-fledged sonata-rondo)[35] as a means of enriching the formal dimensions of the concertante finale while maintaining its bravura content and comic style; innovation, through the assignment of greater weight to the traditionally lightest moments in the concerto, is coupled with conservation.

Brahms's listeners were probably no less musically literate than Mozart's, but their expectations (and Brahms's own compositional pro-

34. See Heinrich Christoph Koch, *Musikalisches Lexicon* (Frankfurt, 1802), cols. 355, 1271–74; Kollmann, *Essay*, 4, 6, 22; Carl Czerny, *School of Practical Composition*, trans. John Bishop, 3 vols. (London: Cocks, [1848]), 1:99, 164; Gustav Schilling, *Encyclopädie der gesammten musikalischen Wissenschaften, oder Universal-Lexicon der Tonkunst* (Stuttgart: Köhler, 1835–38), 2: 288, 6:53–54; and Adolph Bernhard Marx, *Die Lehre von der musikalischen Komposition, Dritter Theil* (Leipzig: Breitkopf & Härtel, 1845), 193.

35. The finales of the C-Major String Quartet, K. 157, and the D-Major Symphony, K. 181, both composed in 1773 (see Malcolm S. Cole, "Sonata-Rondo, the Formulation of a Theoretical Concept in the 18th and 19th Centuries," *Musical Quarterly* 55 [1969]: 182).

clivities) were differently conditioned. If Gustav Jenner was able to state with positive assurance that "Brahms has brought the sonata to life again" (hat die Sonata wieder lebendig gemacht),[36] then the other side of the coin is that, by the late nineteenth century, the sonata (and hence sonata form) was for all intents and purposes a moribund genre; indeed, its death knell had already been sounded, at least in music criticism, by Schumann in the 1830s: "It seems as though the genre [the sonata] has run its life-course, and this is to be sure in the order of things."[37] How then to revivify a genre that threatened to become fit only for musical museum pieces, and how to ensure its dynamic qualities given the propensity of most composers for antidramatic song themes? – these were the questions for which the Mozartean amplified binary provided one possible answer, or at least the musical framework for an answer.

Not surprisingly, then, we find Mozart's form displaced by Brahms into unusual contexts; what had served the earlier composer as a manner of concluding a multimovement cycle might surface at any point in one of the later composer's large-scale works. Michael Musgrave aptly describes the first movement of the G-Minor Piano Quartet (one of Brahms's earliest essays in the Mozartean form) as "the boldest structural experiment Brahms had attempted" and further suggests that here Brahms had to face the knotty problem of balancing its radical structure within the context of the whole work.[38] Brahms solved the immediate problem (and the larger one of intermovement cohesion) by casting the first *and* last movements in essentially the same form; but while the opening Allegro is by turns austere and passionately disruptive, the gypsy Finale strikes a frankly popularizing tone; and while the formal joins in the first movement are smoothed over by the density of the motivic workings, the last movement largely avoids complex thematic development in favor of a more apparently episodic, sectional structure. Many years later, Brahms applied a similar kind of dialectic pairing in the Fourth Symphony, op. 98, this time involving the middle movements. Again, both are sharply contrasted in ethos – the Andante is as expressively lyrical as the Scherzo is boisterous and witty – but they

---

36. Gustav Jenner, *Johannes Brahms als Mensch, Lehrer und Künstler: Studien und Erlebnisse*, 2d ed. (Marburg: Elwert, 1930), 75.

37. *Neue Zeitschrift für Musik* 10 (1839): 134.

38. Musgrave, 96–99.

are bound together by similar constructive traits.[39] In each case – op. 25 and op. 98 – the dual employment of the amplified binary form lends structural coherence to a multimovement work, without Brahms's having to resort to direct thematic recall, thereby answering to a concern that Mozart simply did not have to face.

Formal displacement is further complemented in Brahms by what may be called *generic diffusion*. In the Mozart works that we have considered, the *generic dominant* (to borrow Hans Robert Jauss's term) is clearly the rondo; the majority of Mozart's amplified binaries retain its chief structural feature (the frequent return of the opening music in the tonic) and its comic ethos. In Brahms, the rondo ethos is present as well in some cases – witness the square-cut and relatively easygoing character of the principal themes in the finales of opp. 11, 25, 77, 83, and 111 and the first of the Clarinet Sonatas, op. 120. But, as often as not, comedy is replaced by passionate utterance (as in the opening movements of opp. 25 and 101 or the finales of op. 51, no. 1, and opp. 90 and 108) or, more significantly, recedes in favor of an inward turn toward the lyric (e.g., the slow movement of op. 98 and the finales of opp. 8, 68, and 114). And the lyric impulse manifests itself in less obvious ways as well. In those movements with summarizing codas (especially instances like the finales of opp. 34 and 77, where the coda attains a high degree of self-sufficiency), the amplified binary is further amplified to yield three main form parts: a tonally digressive exposition, an expanded, tonally resolving response, and a compressed restatement that may itself serve a resolving function. In other words, the pattern begins to approach a large-scale series of variations, or, better yet, Lied strophes, and invites comparison with the design of those openly lyrical Brahmsian sonata-form movements in which both development and recapitulation begin with first-group material in the

39. Pascall further points out that even the passacaglia Finale of the symphony integrates elements of the "sonata form with combined response" (i.e., amplified binary) – specifically, a central recapitulatory variation (statement 16 = the passacaglia theme), several developmental variations (statements 17–23), and a resumption of the "recapitulation" (statements 24–26) (see Robert Pascall, "Genre and the Finale of Brahms's Fourth Symphony," *Music Analysis* 8 [1989]: 239–43). Coupled with the fact that, although it is a full-fledged sonata-allegro, the first movement of the symphony features a development section that begins in tonic (thus resembling an amplified binary with summarizing coda [cf. the discussion below]), this means that *all* the symphony's movements play on essentially the same design. I elaborate on this point in chap. 5 of my *Nineteenth-Century Music and the German Romantic Ideology* (New York: Schirmer Books, 1993), 137–44.

tonic: the Finale of the Second Symphony and the first movements of opp. 78, 87, 98, and 120, no. 2.[40] Of course, Brahms's cultivation of the lyric sonata form is mediated by the example of Schubert, who in instances like the opening movement of the G-Major String Quartet, D. 887, reinterpreted the dynamic, goal-directed dialectic of Beethovenian sonata form as a more leisurely, infinitely expandable variation chain.[41] And, as we have seen, the roots of the lyric sonata lie still farther back, in Mozart's amplified binaries with summarizing coda. (Interestingly enough, Heinrich Schenker referred to Brahms in his 1897 obituary as the "Mozart of our day" precisely because of his "characteristic melodic energy.")[42] But while Mozart's lyricism remains at the level of form, Brahms's tends to infuse every detail of the composition. His valuation of the Lied form, as reported by Jenner,[43] thus resonates powerfully in his instrumental works, where it likewise contributes to the diffusion of what were, with Mozart, more strictly limited generic implications. (As a procedural correlate to the diffusion of Mozartean genre traits, we may also cite Brahms's employment of the scattering technique: a device that originally served to address the issue of textural resolution in the concerto became, for Brahms, a more generalized vehicle for motivic cohesion.)

If generic dominants are implicit not only in the works of a particular composer but also in a musical period as a whole, then it might be said that Brahms's age was principally colored by genres that did not figure in his own output: the tone poem and music drama. On the one hand, then, Brahms was apparently out of step with the generic dominants of the latter half of the nineteenth century; he aimed rather to produce "enduring" (*dauerhafte*) music that drew its sustenance from the "laws

40. For an analysis of the first movement of op. 120, no. 2, see Jack Adrian, "The Ternary Sonata Form," *Journal of Music Theory* 34 (1990): 57–80. Although the author finds a precedent for Brahms's "ternary" sonata form in Haydn (Piano Sonata in D, Hob. XVI:51), Mozart's amplified binary would seem to have exerted an even stronger influence. Mozart too wrote "ternary" sonata forms (i.e., with developments beginning in the tonic), for example, the first movement of the Wind Serenade in E♭, K. 375.

41. See Carl Dahlhaus, "Sonata Form in Schubert: The First Movement of the G-Major String Quartet, Op. 161 (D. 887)," trans. Thilo Reinhard, in *Schubert: Critical and Analytical Studies*, ed. Walter Frisch (Lincoln: University of Nebraska Press, 1986), 1–7.

42. Schenker is quoted in Michael Musgrave and Robert Pascall, "The String Quartets Op. 51 No. 1 in C Minor and Op. 51 No. 2 in A Minor: A Preface," in *Brahms* 2, 141.

43. Jenner, *Johannes Brahms als Mensch*, 30.

of pure music" and the spirit of tradition, or so he put it to Jenner.[44] But insofar as Brahms's reach into the past was less a regressive than a re-interpretive and reflective act, his attitude toward genre was remarkably "modern." Formal displacement, generic diffusion – both indicate that Brahms's music partook of one of the more progressive tendencies in nineteenth-century art, the process through which Classical genres were reconfigured as "tones" or qualities. In his divinatory pronouncements on literature, the *Frühromantiker* Friedrich Schlegel already described the transformation of the Classical poetic types – *Lyrik, Epik, Drama* – into the constitutive qualities – *lyrisch, episch, dramatisch* – of the modern genre par excellence, the *Roman*.[45] A similar transformation animates the Brahms works that we have considered. Properly speaking, neither sonata, nor concerto, nor rondo, is magically made *lebendig*; what remains of these historically time-specific entities is a mobile "tone," now divorced from its original generic bonds. If the forms that Brahms appropriated were hardly "modern," the mode of appropriation was eminently so. Which brings us back to Mozart. Was his, as Schoenberg would have it, a "vision of the future"? Yes, to be sure – but only when viewed in tandem with Brahms's complex and refractory dialogue with the past.

44. Ibid., 75–77.

45. See the discussion of this point in Peter Szondi, "Friedrich Schlegel's Theory of Poetical Genres: A Reconstruction from the Posthumous Fragments," in *On Textual Understanding and Other Essays*, trans. Harvey Mendelsohn (Minneapolis: University of Minnesota Press, 1986), 91–94.

APPENDIX

Brahms's careful study of and high praise for the late piano concertos in general, and K. 466 and K. 488 in particular, are well documented, as is his knowledge of the D-Major Flute Concerto, K. 314, and the D-Major Piano Concerto, K. 537. Brahms first performed K. 466 for a Mozart centenary concert on 26 January 1856, and during the years immediately following he conducted performances of K. 453 and K. 488 at the princely court at Detmold. In a letter to Clara Schumann of 7 February 1861, which contains enthusiastic references to K. 491, Brahms wrote, "There is no greater joy than bringing these concertos to life."[46] In addition, Imogen Fellinger reports that Brahms underlined the following entries – perhaps his favorites among the piano concertos – in his copy of the Köchel *Verzeichnis*: K. 450, 453, 466, 467, 482, and 488.[47] Specific references to the rondo Finale of K. 314 and to K. 537 appear, respectively, in Brahms's correspondence from late 1880 with Ernst Rudorff, who at the time was editing the wind concertos for the Breitkopf and Härtel collected edition, and in the reminiscences of Richard Heuberger.[48] We can further point to documentary evidence in support of Brahms's early nurtured fondness for the piano sonatas ("I revel in Mozart's sonatas!" he exclaimed to Clara Schumann in a letter of 5 March 1856) and piano quartets.[49]

As for the chamber music with strings, we can be certain of Brahms's close consideration of the "Haydn" and "Prussian" Quartets, all of which, by his own admission, served as models for his quartet compositions, just as Mozart's String Quintets, K. 515, 516, 593, and 614 figured in the composition of his opp. 88 and 111. In a letter of 24 June 1869 to Simrock, referring to what eventually were published as op. 51, nos. 1 and 2, Brahms noted, "Even Mozart had to work hard in composing six beautiful quartets, so it will be quite a strain for me to make just a couple of passable ones."[50] In a letter to Joachim of 27 November 1890,

---

46. Kalbeck, *Brahms*, 1:255, 3:207; and *Schumann-Brahms Briefe*, 1:239, 355.

47. Fellinger, "Brahms's View of Mozart," 54.

48. *Briefwechsel*, 3:174–77; and Heuberger, *Erinnerungen*, 93.

49. *Schumann-Brahms Briefe*, 1:181; and Kalbeck, *Brahms*, 1:240.

50. *Briefwechsel*, 9:75. On the "Prussian" Quartets, see Kalbeck, *Brahms*, 2:441.

written after the completion of the G-Major String Quintet, op. 111, Brahms told his friend that he should not be reluctant to say so if he found the composition wanting, for, in that case, "I will console myself with the first [the String Quintet, op. 88], and over both [opp. 88 and 111], with Mozart's."[51]

When Brahms scoured the A-Major Piano and Violin Sonata, K. 526, for parallel octaves and fifths, he might well have taken note of its first movement's formal subtleties.[52] The closing movement might have impressed him, too: in the responsive part of the design, the opening forty-two-measure binary unit nearly doubles in length; some of its elements are retained, but are subjected to developmental expansion; others are omitted and replaced by new episodic material; and the tonic/dominant polarity of the opening gives way to an exploration of submediant and subdominant regions. Thus the untroubled *buffa* character of Mozart's initiatory paragraph is deceptive; as in many of Brahms's works, a neatly balanced presentation is countered by an asymmetrical response.

To summarize, of the thirty-five movements from table 4.1, Brahms's direct contact with over a third of them is assured.

51. *Briefwechsel,* 6:256.

52. See Paul Mast, "Brahms's Study, Octaven u. Quinten u. A., with Schenker's Commentary Translated," *Music Forum* 5 (1980): 1–196; and Fellinger, "Brahms's View of Mozart," 44.

FIVE

Brahms's Cello Sonata in F Major and Its Genesis: A Study in Half-Step Relations

Margaret Notley

A mystery connects Brahms's Cello Sonata in F Major, op. 99, to his earlier Cello Sonata in E Minor, op. 38. Brahms's handwritten entries in his personal inventory of works indicate that he had completed three movements of the E-minor work in 1862 and a fourth movement in June 1865.[1] Yet, when in June 1866 this sonata appeared in print, it contained only three movements, with two Allegros surrounding an Allegretto quasi Menuetto. Max Kalbeck speculated that the discarded slow movement – "which Brahms had laid aside because he did not want to overload the work" – may have reappeared in 1886, more than twenty years later, as the Adagio affettuoso of the F-Major Sonata.[2]

I would like to thank Professors Timothy Jackson, Robert P. Morgan, Leon Plantinga, and James Webster for their comments on earlier versions of this essay. I would also like to thank John Gingerich for our discussions regarding cello technique; Richard Boursy and Professor Stephen Hinton for offering editorial suggestions; and Dr. Otto Biba and the staff of the GdM for allowing me extended access to the autograph of op. 99.

1. Orel, 536.

2. Kalbeck, *Brahms*, 4:33. (Unless otherwise noted, all translations are mine.) Brahms's habit of reusing thematic material from earlier compositions, indeed, even entire compositions themselves, is well known. Among many studies, see James Webster, "The C Sharp Minor Version of Brahms's Op. 60," *Musical Times* 121 (1980): 89–93; Robert Pascall, "Brahms's *Missa canonica* and Its Recomposition in His Motet 'Warum' Op. 74 No. 1," in *Brahms*, 111–36, and "Unknown Gavottes by Brahms," *Music and Letters* 57 (1976): 404–11.

Kalbeck is by no means an infallible critic of Brahms's music; this time, however, he seems right on target when, continuing, he says that the "heavenly Adagio [of op. 99] arouses the feeling that it is the soul of the work, which now had to fashion for itself its body."[3] This proposition implies a corollary: the nature of the preexisting Adagio would have influenced the shape of the movements that Brahms may have subsequently composed around it. As we shall see, support for both propositions – as well as for Kalbeck's view that the Adagio of op. 99 derives from the rejected slow movement of op. 38 – is provided by both music-analytical and philological evidence. But, before surveying these clues, we must consider the broader issue of Brahms's use of Neapolitan relationships, for these constitute a significant link between the two sonatas.

I

Christopher Wintle has recently discussed Brahms's use in his sonata-form movements of the "Neapolitan complex" of relationships, expanded "to absorb, and accommodate itself to, the traditional form-defining opposition of tonic and dominant."[4] Following Arnold Schoenberg's lead, Wintle invokes the "duality offered by the tonic major/minor alternation" and finds that, in a number of pieces, Brahms drew on a specific group of key relations: tonic major/minor, dominant major/minor, (flat) submediant, and Neapolitan major/minor. The first movement of op. 38 is a case in point. Wintle notes the importance of the half-step motion between $\hat{6}$ and $\hat{5}$ in the opening melodic gesture, and he charts Brahms's gradual deployment of the Neapolitan-related set of keys. The keys of the transition and second group are C major (VI), B minor (v), and B major (V), which become F major (♮II), E minor (i), and E major (I) in the recapitulation. Wintle sees F minor (♮ii), the final key of the set, as emerging, "almost inevitably," to become "the goal, from every point of view, of the development section."

As James Webster has demonstrated, semitonal relationships also pervade the first movement of the Piano Quintet in F Minor, op. 34.[5]

3. Kalbeck, *Brahms*, 4:33. Michael Musgrave concurs that "it is the slow movement which may be seen as carrying the main emotional weight of the work" (Musgrave, 194).

4. Christopher Wintle, "The 'Sceptred Pall': Brahms's Progressive Harmony," in *Brahms 2*, 197–222; in this paragraph, I quote from pp. 199 and 207.

5. James Webster, "Schubert's Sonata Form and Brahms's First Maturity (II)," *19th-Century*

Throughout the movement, melodic and accompanimental materials alike emphasize the interval of a half step. To be sure, this movement does not draw on the full array of keys that Wintle describes. But Brahms has chosen C♯ minor (vi) and D♭ major (VI) as secondary keys, and in both the exposition and the recapitulation of the second group he introduces keys locally related by half step. Because of these tonal relationships and, even more, the extraordinary emphasis placed on the $\hat{6}$–$\hat{5}$ and other *melodic* half-step relationships, this movement, too, can be said to be organized around Neapolitan relations.

The Adagio affettuoso of the F-Major Cello Sonata is in F♯ major, the key of the Neapolitan major. Internally, this slow movement, a binary/ternary hybrid, features what Tovey called the "inverse" Neapolitan relationship (here F minor to F♯ major), which Wintle sees as "both problematic and puzzling":[6]

mm.:	1–19	20–44	44–63	63–71
	A	B	A′	coda
key:	F♯ → C♯	f/D♭	F♯ → D → F♯	F♯/f♯

Brahms's emphasis on melodic semitonal relations rather than on the complete set of Neapolitan key relationships recalls his compositional concerns in op. 34 more closely than those in op. 38. That the Adagio affetuoso is not a sonata-form first movement, however, sets his exploration of these relationships here apart from those undertaken in either of the other movements. As we shall see, the taut, idiosyncratic form of the movement is intimately connected with Brahms's development of the inverse Neapolitan relationship.

The melodic pitches of a Neapolitan progression in F minor, G♭–E♮–F, constitute an Ur-motive for this movement in F♯ major. The pitches first appear, written as F♯–E♮–E♯, in m. 2 (ex. 5.1). The V[7]/IV in this measure is surprising, and the cello's E♯ clashes with the E♮ of the piano. The treble then takes up the E♯–F♯ motion from the cello, in this way initiating the tangled imitative counterpoint characteristic of this movement.

Music 3 (1979): 65–68. Brahms completed an earlier version of the piano quintet scored for string quintet in 1862, the same year in which he wrote the original first three movements of the E-Minor Cello Sonata.

6. Tovey, "Tonality in Schubert," in *Main Stream*, 148–49; Wintle, "The 'Sceptred Pall,' " 203.

Example 5.1: Op. 99, 2d mvt., mm. 1–19.

The possibilities for changes in the relative stability between pitches a semitone apart, as well as for unorthodox resolutions, especially between these three melodic pitches, soon become a central topic of the discourse. Throughout the A section (mm. 1–19), Brahms presents the tonic, dominant, and subdominant chords as languid rivals, and the melodic notes F♯–E♯–E♮ figure prominently in the harmonic events. Despite the subdominant implication of V^7/IV (under the treble E♮) in m. 2, the various contrapuntal strands of the first phrase come together in m. 4 on a more conventional tonicized dominant (under a stressed melodic E♯).

The second phrase opens unexpectedly on the subdominant (m. 5), and Brahms sets this phrase up to be harmonically, as well as thematically, parallel to the first (see ex. 5.1). The two phrases, in fact, form a closed, if harmonically unusual, period (I → V, IV → I), but Brahms expands the consequent by increasing the emphasis on the subdominant. He repeats the V^7/VII of m. 6 (paralleling the V^7/IV of m. 2), rather than resolving it immediately; a chromatic ascent with a crescendo by the cello makes the regained V^7/I in m. 8 seem decisive, but at this climax of the entire section E♯ collapses onto E♮ supported by V^7/IV. The eventual full cadence that closes the period (m. 12) simultaneously initiates a new phrase in which a weak modulation to the dominant (C♯) occurs (m. 16). As a part of the tonicized C♯-major triad, the pitch E♯ is now more stable than F♯, a shift in stability emphasized by the treble F♯–E♯ motion in m. 19 (see ex. 5.1).

The opening of the B section reveals the meaning of this shift; Brahms inverts the notes C♯ and E♯ and reinterprets them enharmonically (ex. 5.2). Within the notated key, D♭ becomes unstable in relation to C, and it resolves immediately, albeit temporarily, to C in the opening mo-

Example 5.2.

tive played by the cello (m. 20). The ensuing passage is marked by a
struggle between D♭ major, the tonicized dominant of F♯ major, and F
minor, which is represented by *its* dominant. The question is whether
the pitches D♭ and C represent $\hat{6}$–$\hat{5}$ in F minor or, in reverse order, $\hat{7}$–$\hat{1}$
in D♭ major.

Brahms organizes the first part of the new section around two roughly
equivalent statements of a circular bass line (mm. 20–24, 24–28). The
plunging line of the cello in m. 24 places the D♭–C motion in the bass.
The resulting cadential six-four chord in F minor resolves quickly: the
important half-step motion, F–E♮ in the piano treble, derives from the
Ur-motive. But the bass line's cycle has already begun again. Changes
toward the end of the cycle and new, rhapsodic passagework in the piano
make a second arrival on a six-four chord (m. 28) more emphatic, but
this resolves even less satisfactorily, and the key shifts back to D♭ major
(mm. 30 ff.). Despite the key signature, F minor has only tentatively been
established through its dominant; the tenuous C♯ (D♭) major at the end
of the A section has been succeeded by a more unstable F minor. Brahms
has composed beautifully detailed moment-to-moment ambiguities. In
the larger context, however, it seems that the bass of the F-minor V$^{6\text{-}5}_{4\text{-}3}$ is
just an expanded lower-neighbor note in the prevailing D♭ major.

In his description of this section, Kalbeck again shows unusual sen-
sitivity: "One can no longer speak here of *a* melody; everything has
become melody, even the middle voices and the bass, and they flow into
each other in melancholy interpenetration."[7] Brahms has associated
certain melodic half-step relationships with a conflict between two keys.
It is this harmonic situation, together with his mastery of the contrapuntal possibilities of the cello-piano medium, that allows the composer
to create the continuous melody.

At the point where the D♭–C conflict is resolved more or less defini-
tively in favor of D♭ (m. 33), thematic fragments from the opening of the
movement reappear in the bass line (ex. 5.3). Here Brahms invokes the
dominant-seventh/augmented-sixth ambiguity so frequently used by

Example 5.3: Op. 99, 2d mvt., mm. 31–39.

Classical and Romantic composers. The prolonged $D\flat^7$ (mm. 37–39)
could be a German-sixth chord in F minor – it follows a sequence (mm.
35–37) that has ended on an F-minor triad – but the broader harmonic
setting (from m. 31) makes $G\flat$ ($F\sharp$) major more likely. Rather than concluding the B section by resolving the $D\flat^7$ ($C\sharp^7$) directly to $F\sharp$ major, however, Brahms moves deceptively to an apparent D^7 chord (prolonged in
mm. 40–42), the German-sixth chord in the key of $F\sharp$. This leads, in the
expected manner, to a cadential six-four chord in m. 43 and then to the
varied reprise of A.

Although the A and the B sections explore different harmonic rela-
tionships, the crucial pitches $F\sharp$–$E\sharp$–$E\natural$ ($G\flat$–$F\natural$–$E\natural$) recur, with several
changes in meaning, in the same (treble) register of the piano at for-
mally significant points in both: at the local climax in m. 8 ($E\sharp$–$E\natural$), at
the $C\sharp$-major close in m. 19 ($F\sharp$–$E\sharp$), at the critical moment where $D\flat$
moves to C in the bass in m. 24 ($F\natural$–$E\natural$) – this is where the two statements

7. Kalbeck, *Brahms*, 4:34.

of the circular bass overlap – and in m. 28 when the F-minor six-four chord is reconfirmed as a structural sonority in the B section (F♮) before the motion back toward D♭ and then G♭ (F♯) major.

Brahms continues to develop the implications of his thematic material in the reprise, as the events in the central section affect the course of the material that follows. In mm. 51–53, the harmonic divagations that had first appeared in mm. 8–10 actually lead somewhere and now become part of a modulation to ♭VI (D major). The relationship between D major and F♯ major recreates the relationship between D♭ (C♯) major and F minor that had connected the A and B sections and pervaded the latter; not only does Brahms resolve the modulation to the dominant (C♯/D♭) that had occurred at the end of the opening section by ending the reprise in the tonic key, but he also "resolves" the (frustrated) modulation from C♯ (D♭) to F minor that had originally led to the middle section. Here the replication and resolution of the third relationship (D♭–f becomes D–F♯) resembles Brahms's recapitulatory practice in harmonically complicated sonata-form movements, and, in retrospect, it strengthens the connection between the A and the B sections.[8] Brahms enhances this effect in the coda (mm. 63–71) by drawing together in one phrase thematic materials from both the A and the B sections.

Semitonal relationships and the often wayward resolutions associated with them are thus central to the form – and expressive effect – of the Adagio affettuoso. Brahms has based the unusual structure of the A and B sections on two tentative modulations. Ternary-form slow movements traditionally included an agitated, harmonically unsettled middle sec-

8. As Elaine Sisman has noted, "In Brahms's slow movements, one must always mediate between the received musical messages and their unexpected resolutions – a step-by-step process – and the larger sections and their assigned weights and relationships – a retrospective process" (See "Brahms's Slow Movements: Re-inventing the 'Closed' Forms," in *Brahms Studies*, 102).

I am grateful to Timothy Jackson for pointing out to me that A′ opens on a V$^{6-5}_{4-3}$ (m. 44) and that the dominant prolongation at the end of the B section thus continues into the reprise. (And the first phrase of A′, like that of A, closes on a tonicized dominant [m. 47].) The projection of the key (F♯) through its dominant here intensifies the harmonic parallel with the B section. I would like to thank Professor Jackson as well for showing me that the pitches C–D♭, which are so significant in the B section, also play a prominent role, as B♯–C♯, in the outer sections of the movement: the B♯ repeatedly moves as a chromatic passing tone between IV and V (e.g., in the bass in mm. 9 and 11) to help "set straight" the relationship between the two chords.

tion, and he has given this traditional feature a new significance through the sonata's special focus on half-step relations. But he sets up the harmonic situation for the B section by means of a (weak) modulation to the dominant, that is, by taking on the characteristic feature of major-mode binary forms. Despite the apparently great distance between the keys of the two sections, they connect together smoothly because of changes in the status and meaning of melodic half-step relationships. The reprise recapitulates the harmonic events associated with the exploration of half-step relationships in the opening A and B sections. Melodic half-step relationships have formal significance here, and the composer's use of them makes the rich and varied harmonic language coherent across the individual sections of the movement.

* * *

In its opulent, Schubertian harmonic style, the Adagio affettuoso perhaps stands closer to Brahms's works from the early 1860s than to those from the mid-1880s – which, of course, would support the possibility that this piece might be the missing slow movement of op. 38.[9] To be sure, Ivor Keys has questioned Kalbeck's conjectured relationship between the two sonatas on account of the Adagio's "tonal surprises," in particular, the appearance of an F-minor section within the key of F♯ major. But this "surprise" is perfectly in keeping with Brahms's preoccupation during the period of his "first maturity" with Neapolitan relationships.[10] We have seen that he drew on them in the first movements of opp. 34 and 38; he explored them as well in the slow movements of the Piano Quartet in A (op. 26, completed 1861) and the String Sextet in G (op. 36, from 1864–65). The inverse Neapolitan relationship, too,

9. This movement can profitably be compared with the Adagio of Schubert's C-Major String Quintet, a piece that Brahms came to know well in the early 1860s. The A sections of Schubert's ternary-form slow movement are in E major, while the middle section is in the Neapolitan-related key of F minor. The B section of this movement, like that of Brahms's Adagio affettuoso, is formed around a circular chord progression and a thwarted modulation. Schubert's progression repeatedly takes a D♭-major chord, ostensibly VI in F minor, as the Neapolitan in C minor. Although the motion toward C minor becomes progressively stronger, the modulation is never completed.

10. Ivor Keys, *Johannes Brahms* (London: Christopher Helm, 1989), 220. As Ira Braus has argued, "Save for op. 99 and possibly op. 98/II, Brahms indeed abandons [the Neapolitan complex] after 1870. The N-complex, therefore, may be metaphorical for the 'Sturm und Drang' phase of Brahms's personal and artistic history" (review of *Brahms 2, Journal of Music Theory* 34 [1990]: 115).

appears in another instrumental work from this period: Brahms composed an A♭-major second theme in the A-minor slow movement of the Serenade in A (op. 16, from 1858–59).

As I suggested above, the emphasis on melodic semitonal relationships connects this movement to the first movement of the Piano Quintet in particular. But Brahms had also focused on the ♭$\hat{6}$–$\hat{5}$ relationship in the first movement of op. 38, and his fascination in the first half of the 1860s with the *ambiguities* possible in the $\hat{6}$–$\hat{5}$ relationship is especially evident in the first movement of the G-Major String Sextet. Although he works with the same melodic and key relationships in the Adagio affettuoso, the extreme tightness in the form shows the hand of the older Brahms.[11] It is likely, therefore, that, if Brahms has reused the earlier movement in op. 99, he has revised it. The manuscript evidence to support the derivation of the Adagio affettuoso from the Adagio of op. 38 is slender but suggestive.

II

No holograph of op. 38 is extant. The *Stichvorlage* comprised an autograph of the first movement and a copyist's manuscript of the remaining two movements (the Allegretto quasi Menuetto and the final Allegro that appear in the published version), but these sources have disappeared.[12] Brahms may have destroyed the autograph of the original second, third, and fourth movements at the time of publication. Because he was in the habit of reusing unpublished compositions, however, it seems likely that he would have held on to the autograph of the rejected slow movement at least.

Like most of Brahms's extant manuscripts, the autograph of op. 99 is a fair copy rather than a working draft. Brahms does not often leave clues that invite meaningful interpretation, but this autograph contains several interesting revisions and a divergence from his usual practice in putting together a manuscript. The structure of the gathering indicates that he may have copied the second movement separately from the rest

11. Critics, including the very earliest ones, have invariably remarked on the new conciseness in the chamber pieces from the mid-1880s. In his account of op. 99, for example, Alfred von Ehrmann terms the slow movement a piece "of exemplary compactness" (*Johannes Brahms: Weg, Werk und Welt* [Leipzig: Breitkopf & Härtel, 1933], 378).

12. See McCorkle, 137. The publisher, N. Simrock, apparently received a copy of the Adagio as well; this engraver's model may have survived into the 1930s (see George S. Bozarth, "Paths Not Taken: The 'Lost' Works of Johannes Brahms," *Music Review* 50 [1989]: 189).

of the autograph. Given the unknown fate of the Adagio originally part of the earlier sonata, this is potentially of some significance.

Brahms wrote his chamber music on oblong paper, most typically in continuous nested pairs of bifolios. He rarely separated the movements by beginning each on a new leaf or bifolio, and he was even in the habit of beginning a new movement, with no empty systems between, on the same page on which he had finished the previous one.[13] But Brahms has not continuously paired the bifolios of the op. 99 manuscript, nor does it systematically show his usual parsimony: two bifolios for the first movement (eight pages, with the last half page empty), a *separate* bifolio for the second movement (four pages, with the last half page also empty), and three bifolios (two nested bifolios followed by one separate bifolio, a total of twelve pages) for the third and fourth movements (each movement fills six pages). The reason for the separation of the first movement from the rest of the manuscript is known: during the summer of 1886, Brahms sent the first movements of four chamber works (opp. 99, 100, 101, and 108) to his friend Theodor Billroth for copying.[14] In no extant manuscript of a chamber work other than the autographs of opp. 18 and 78 does Brahms detach a movement from the rest of the manuscript as he does the first and second movements of op. 99. This fact suggests strongly that Brahms prepared the Adagio affettuoso apart from the other movements.

Brahms need not have copied the Adagio affettuoso separately from the other movements simply because he had reworked earlier material. Although the slow movements of both the G-Major String Sextet and the F-Major String Quintet – completed, respectively, in 1865 and 1882 – use material that dates from the 1850s, Brahms has not separated either movement within its manuscript, nor would there have been any clear reason for him to have done so. There *would* be a reason, however, if he had revised the earlier slow movement and then transposed it as he

13. For a detailed discussion of Brahms's chamber-music autographs, see the appendix.

14. See Brahms's letter to Billroth of 8 August 1886 and Billroth's reply of 18 August, in *Billroth und Brahms*, 396. The complete autographs of opp. 99 and 101 are in the GdM. The autograph of the first movement of op. 100, complete but for the last twelve measures, is in the Biblioteka Jagiellońska, Cracow; the autograph for the remaining movements of op. 100 and the entire autograph of op. 108 are missing. The first movement of op. 101 fills twelve pages of two pairs of nested bifolios (there is unused space at the bottom of the page), and the second movement follows on the thirteenth page. Brahms evidently cut through the second pair of bifolios in order to send this first movement to Billroth.

copied it for the manuscript of op. 99: transposition is a separate task that would have involved the whole movement here but no other part of the sonata.

Since the E-Minor Cello Sonata (op. 38) also deals with Neapolitan relationships, and since the Adagio affettuoso stands in the key of F♯ major within the F-Major Cello Sonata (op. 99), the natural key to consider is F major, which would have placed the original slow movement in the Neapolitan relationship to the overall key of op. 38. Several additional considerations tend to support F major as the key of the earlier movement. This sort of transposition requires the composer to change only the key signature and accidentals, which makes it an obvious first choice; more important, only a slight change in range is involved.[15] The earlier sonata, furthermore, does not demand nearly as much of the cellist as the second sonata, and transposing the movement to F major puts it on a level of technical difficulty more in line with that of the three published movements of op. 38. (It also significantly alters the character of the movement, giving it a much less edgy lyricism.) Finally, one extremely odd revision seems to imply that Brahms used precisely this transposition in copying the Adagio affettuoso.

Karl Geiringer observed that, for a late manuscript by Brahms, the autograph of op. 99 contains an unusually large number of revisions.[16] Within this heavily revised autograph, the second movement stands out as almost clean. The only significant revision occurs in m. 24 when the D♭ in the cello resolves to C (ex. 5.4). Brahms twice wrote a D♭ octave for the cello. He immediately scribbled out with ink the first D♭ octave and the note or notes that followed it (it is not possible to read what follows just after the D♭ octave, but most likely there was originally a C octave on the second beat). He probably did not cross out the upper note of the

15. It is well known that Bach used this sort of transposition to complete the sets of the *Well-Tempered Clavier*. There is also an interesting parallel in Haydn sources. The Adagio cantabile in F♯ major from the F♯-Minor Piano Trio (Hob. XV:26) is identical to the Adagio in F major from the Symphony No. 102 in B♭ Major. Most early critics believed the slow movement of the trio to be an arrangement of that of the symphony, but more recent commentators have concluded that the version in the piano trio predates that in the symphony (see the preface to Joseph Haydn, *Klaviertrios: 3. Folge*, ed. Irmgard Becker-Gulach [Munich: G. Henle Verlag, 1986]). And Brahms himself had used this sort of transposition both when he adapted the same material for a vocal quartet ("Der Gang zum Liebchen," op. 31, no. 3, in E♭) and a waltz (op. 39, no. 5, in E) and when he recomposed parts of his early C♯-Minor Piano Quartet for the Piano Quartet in C Minor, op. 60.

16. Geiringer, 239.

Example 5.4: Op. 99, 2d mvt., m. 24 (diplomatic transcription
of the autograph).

second D♭ octave until later, first, because he has finished writing in the details of rhythmic notation in ink and, second, because he has crossed out the upper D♭ in pencil. (He also later added the slur beneath the bass notes D♭–C in pencil.) The revisions in this measure are striking – especially because of the stumbling implied by the repetition of the pair of octaves – since Brahms has already worked out compositional problems elsewhere in the movement; as noted above, the autograph of this movement is otherwise very clean. He seems to be grappling with a new possibility on the spot.

The proposed level of transposition is *upward* from F major (E minor in the B section) to F♯ major (F minor in the B section). Under those circumstances, Brahms would not have been obliged to check the range before transposing; not fewer notes but rather one *more* note would have been available in the transposed key. He might not, then, have thought out m. 24 in the new key before he began to transpose and copy it simultaneously into the extant autograph. (The premise is that the composer had previously reworked the earlier Adagio, still in F major, in his preserved autograph. That would explain the cleanness of the extant autograph for the slow movement of op. 99: he had already revised the movement.) As the first place in the movement in which Brahms uses the lower limit of the cello, the open C string, m. 24 is the first measure unplayable, as published in F♯ major, in the key of F major (E minor in the B section).

Two hypothetical earlier versions seem possible (ex. 5.5). Version B is much more likely. The passage leading up to m. 24 has the six-four chord on the second beat as its goal; in version A, the C octave with its resonant open string would have placed too much emphasis on the preceding chord. According to the proposed scenario, after transposing the original notes of version B, Brahms would have realized that he could now double the important half-step motive in the lower octave. Perhaps he crossed out the first pair of octaves because of the unusualness of the writing, specifically, the D♭ octave: composers rarely write

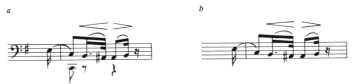

Example 5.5: *a*, Version A. *b*, Version B.

octaves in first position on the cello unless one of the notes can be played on an open string. But these consecutive octaves are by no means impossible to play, and Brahms decided to use them. Later, he presumably removed the upper D♭ of the first octave because it is the bass of the six-four chord that is more enhanced by octave reinforcement in this passage and because the descending tenth to the low D♭ – not musically possible before – makes a more effective gesture than the D♭ octave.

All this is speculative, of course; yet this hypothesis offers an explanation for an otherwise mystifying revision. Why else would Brahms not have thought of the octaves or, at least, the C octave under the six-four chord before? If only the D♭ octave was a new idea, why did he scribble out both, completely obliterating the C octave? To be sure, two other passages for the cello in the Adagio affettuoso as it stands would have been impossible in the key of F major: the lower notes C in mm. 27–28 (the second C, again, as part of an important six-four chord) and the lower notes B♯ in m. 64. But both passages follow m. 24, and, after his experience in transposing m. 24, Brahms would have been fully aware of the new possibilities.

The circumstantial evidence in support of the derivation of the Adagio affettuoso from the missing Adagio of op. 38, then, is strong: a lack of manuscript evidence that would weaken the possibility (Brahms did not send the *autograph* of all four movements of the first sonata to the publisher); the separation of the Adagio affettuoso within the autograph of op. 99; one very puzzling revision in the autograph of the Adagio; and a harmonic style in the Adagio consistent with that of Brahms's works from the 1860s, in particular, the exploration of Neapolitan relationships in both cello sonatas.

III

Arnold Schoenberg was not the first commentator to notice the key relationships that unify all movements of op. 99, but his remarks are the best known: "One is surprised to find the second movement in F♯ major, only to discover later that F major and f minor are contrastingly connected with F♯ (G♭) major and f♯ minor in all four movements."[17] Thus the development of the opening movement, an F-major Allegro vivace, begins in F♯ minor. The third movement, a scherzo in F minor, includes an F-major trio in binary form; the modulatory passage after its first double bar briefly establishes G♭. (The scherzo itself also momentarily tonicizes F♯ minor, but Brahms does nothing to highlight the passage.) And the F-major Finale, a rondo with an A B A C A′ B′ A shape, features a reprise of the refrain in G♭ after the central episode. Here, as if from another world, the Ur-motive reappears three times. The first statement (mm. 54–56) sets off the exploration of flat-side harmonies that marks the rest of the movement; two consecutive statements of the Ur-motive (mm. 77–79, 80–82) later lead with a slightly enigmatic logic to the G♭-major statement of the refrain.

But if Brahms thus justifies and poeticizes the appearance of the Neapolitan key in each of the other three movements, in none does he examine half-step relations in the same degree of detail as in the slow movement. With this difference comes the implication that the Adagio affettuoso served as a preexisting core around which Brahms created the striking pattern of key relationships in the other movements.

How, then, would the Adagio affettuoso have fit into op. 38? Motivic connections make the hypothetical F-major version of the slow movement plausible as part of the earlier sonata. There are two sets of semitonal relationships in the Adagio affettuoso: the Ur-motive (F♯–E♯–E♮) and the D♭–C motive of the B section. In F major, these become F–E–E♭ and C–B. Wintle has described two half-step relationships as central in op. 38: the C–B motive in the opening theme of the first movement and the F–E relationship that pervades the A-minor Allegretto quasi Menuetto.[18] The E-minor middle section of the putative F-major Adagio would have further explored the C–B motive that is so prominent in the first theme – and coda – of the Allegro non troppo. With its initial F–E

---

17. Arnold Schoenberg, *Structural Functions of Harmony*, ed. Leonard Stein (New York: W. W. Norton & Co., 1969), 73. Edwin Evans noticed the complete pattern, too, applying the terms *semitonic rise* and *semitonic fall* to Brahms's use of these tonal relations (see *A Handbook to the Chamber and Orchestral Music of Johannes Brahms*, 3 vols. [London: W. Reeves (1935)], 3:176, 178, 182n, 183; see also Emil Krause, *Johannes Brahms in seinen Werken: Eine Studie, mit Verzeichnissen sämtlicher Instrumental- und Vokal-Kompositionen des Meisters* [Hamburg: Lucas Gräfe & Sillem, 1892], 51; and A[dolf] Steiner, "Johannes Brahms," *Neujahrsblatt der Allgemeinen Musikgesellschaft in Zürich* 87 [1899]: 20).

18. See Wintle, " 'The Sceptred Pall,' " pp. 206–7, 210.

motion in the piano treble, the Allegretto quasi Menuetto would have taken up the first two notes of the Ur-motive, and the opening motive would have sounded natural after the closing F-major chord of the slow movement.

The A-minor Allegretto quasi Menuetto would, in fact, have followed an F-major version of the Adagio affettuoso more smoothly and effectively than it follows the first movement of op. 38. But in other respects the F-major Adagio causes problems of balance in a hypothetically reconstructed four-movement version of op. 38. The motivic connections among the movements are, if anything, too obtrusive. Moreover, two relatively short movements follow two lengthy movements. Placing the interior movements in reverse order does not improve the balance; the sequence of movements, furthermore, seems unnatural.

But the real problem lies between the Allegro non troppo and the hypothetical F-major Adagio, for in several important respects they are too much alike. Both are based on long (but nonetheless extensively developed) melodies, and both draw on virtually the same set of keys: the first movement uses the full set of Neapolitan key relations (E major/minor, B major/minor, C major, F major/minor); the F-major Adagio would have been structured around the keys of F major/minor, C major, E minor, and D♭ major. According to Kalbeck, Brahms removed the Adagio from op. 38 because that sonata seemed "too stuffed full with music."[19] If the Adagio affettuoso does derive from the Adagio of the E-Minor Sonata, then Brahms's task in reviving the suppressed movement as a part of the second cello sonata would have been clear: to deploy Neapolitan relationships in the new movements in a more varied, less heavy-handed manner and to compose movements around the imposing slow movement that would balance better with it. The challenge of composing a first movement that could effectively precede the Adagio affettuoso might well account for certain idiosyncratic features in the Allegro vivace of op. 99.

* * *

The F-Major Cello Sonata appeared, along with the Violin Sonata in A Major, op. 100, and Piano Trio in C Minor, op. 101, in the 1886–87 season. The cello sonata as a whole was seen by one reviewer as "singular," by another as "a work rich in thought, of intimate beauties, that

19. Kalbeck, *Brahms*, 2:191.

does not willingly make itself accessible to every listener and doubtless, as well, not with the first hearing." Eduard Hanslick compared op. 99 with op. 100 and found the violin sonata to be the "lighter, more popular" of the two; the cello sonata he described as having an "agitated and musically more complex nature."[20]

The first movement of op. 99 was to one reviewer the "most singular"; to another, a movement in which "many of the intermediate links remain unclear to the unprepared listener."[21] Tovey later described certain of its features as "peculiar," while Hans Mersmann noted that "the musical language of the composer becomes here completely subjective (not as to content, but as to style)," adding that this subjective style "gives rise to a design that avoids every firmly imprinted shape."[22]

Although the movement is in sonata form, many passages sound freely constructed, almost extemporized. Billroth seems to have had this in mind, as also the related quality of agitated drama, when, in a letter of October 1886, he wrote Brahms that the beginning of the sonata "is almost dangerously *à la* Rubinstein."[23] The first theme, frag-

20. "dr. h.p." (Hans Paumgartner), writing in the *Wiener Abendpost* (a supplement to the *Wiener Zeitung*) of 30 November 1886: "m.s.," writing in the *Pester Lloyd* of 23 December 1886; and Eduard Hanslick, writing in the *Neue Freie Presse* of 7 December 1886. Hanslick's review later appeared in the collection *Musikalisches und Litterarisches: Kritiken und Schilderungen*, vol. 5 of *Die moderne Oper* (Berlin: Allgemeiner Verein für deutschen Literatur, 1889); it was translated by Susan Gillespie as "Brahms's Newest Instrumental Compositions (1889)," in *Brahms and His World*, ed. Walter Frisch (Princeton, N.J.: Princeton University Press, 1990), 146.

21. "ck.," writing in the *Neue Berliner Musikzeitung* of 31 March 1887; Theodor Helm, writing in the *Deutsche Zeitung* (morning edition) of 27 November 1886. Schoenberg asserted that "at the time of Brahms's death this sonata was still very unpopular and was considered indigestible" because of its unusual opening theme (see Arnold Schoenberg, "The Orchestral Variations, Op. 31: A Radio Talk," translated in *The Score* 27 [1960]: 28; see also Walter Frisch's discussion of Schoenberg's analysis in *Brahms and the Principle of Developing Variation* [Berkeley and Los Angeles: University of California Press, 1984], 4–5 and 146–47).

22. Tovey, "Brahms's Chamber Music," in *Main Stream*, 260; Hans Mersmann, *Deutsche Romantik*, vol. 3 of *Die Kammermusik* (Leipzig: Breitkopf & Härtel, 1930), 111.

23. *Billroth und Brahms*, 407. A contemporaneous critic wrote about the problematic nature of Anton Rubinstein's chamber music: "Anyone who understands Rubinstein's artistic temperament more completely will not be surprised by the problematic nature of his chamber music. For the degree of concentration essential here is seldom granted to him. To roll stones from a cliff and let them thunder down into the valley is not difficult for him. But to square them with difficulty, to chisel them with all architectural scrupulousness, that he does not bring himself to do so easily. Concentration and sculptural meticulousness, however, are matters of importance in precisely this artistic genre" ([Adolf] Bernhard Vogel, *Anton Rubinstein: Bio-*

mented and disjointed, is strikingly unlike any other sonata-form theme that Brahms ever wrote. "The broken rhythm of the main theme," Tovey noted, "and the ways in which it is transformed into sustained figures in the course of development constitute a notable addition to the resources of sonata style." Throughout the movement, the opening material seems to be striving for a conventional thematic shape, which constantly eludes it.[24]

The development section, too, occupies a special position among Brahms's sonata forms. Arno Mitschka noted that Brahms's "point of departure . . . was the Romantic treatment of the development section" and observed that "in [the music of] all the Romantics, episodic elements stand out, especially lyrical episodes, improvisatory passages or remembrance-motives, whose sudden rising to the surface or whose reappearance is not architecturally but associatively justified." Mitschka saw Brahms's development sections as standing from the beginning between the Classical and the Romantic models, between the "rational method of motivic work and development" of Beethoven and what Mitschka considered to be the "irrational" treatment of this part of the form by Schubert and Schumann.[25]

The development section of op. 99 is unique in Brahms's œuvre in its thoroughgoing use of the "Romantic" procedures that Mitschka describes. After the allusion – in a Neapolitan-related key – to the opening of the exposition in mm. 66–74, the style becomes improvisatory, the only (loose) connections with thematic material being the chromatic passagework in sixteenth notes and, perhaps, a very hidden reference to the exposition's opening fourth in the following, and other, analogous passages (ex. 5.6).[26] The "sudden rising to the surface" of an

---

graphischer Abriß nebst Charakteristik seiner Werke, vol. 5 of *Musikheroen der Neuzeit* [Leipzig: Max Hesse, 1888], 39).

24. Tovey, "Brahms's Chamber Music," 260. According to Mersmann (*Deutsche Romantik*, 110–11), the movement "is dominated by thrusting short motives that resist every firm binding"; the "sustained figures" that Tovey mentions never achieve the coherence of most tonal sonata-form themes.

25. Arno Mitschka, *Der Sonatensatz in den Werken von Johannes Brahms* (Gütersloh, 1961), 155, 156, 143, 156.

26. Michael Musgrave refers also to "an improvisatory, almost fantasy-like development section which appears after the formal opening transition" (Musgrave, 194). Roger Graybill offers an interesting interpretation for Brahms's use of the Neapolitan-related key here (see "Harmonic Circularity in Brahms's F Major Cello Sonata: An Alternative to Schenker's Read-

Example 5.6: Op. 99, 1st mvt., mm. 74–75.

explicit fourth in m. 94 is dramatic, almost melodramatic – note the cello's tremolos, the high register of the piano, the *pianissimo* marking – and "associatively" rather than "architecturally" justified; it is as if, in the midst of all the free passagework, the head motive is suddenly remembered (and this remembrance initiates the retransition). In none of its parts does the development section elaborate motivic material in a systematic fashion: instead, it creates a Romantic, fantastical atmosphere.

Brahms uses a diffuse, improvisatory style in several transitional passages as well. Edwin Evans considered the exposition's transition (specifically mm. 21–33) "a blemish . . . incongruous and gloomy."[27] The slackening of tension is, in fact, unusual in this part of a sonata form; on the other hand, transitional passages are an obvious choice for fantasy-like writing. At the end of the development, Brahms makes a similar effect in the short passage after the premature reappearance of the augmented first theme in the tonic (mm. 119–23).

In the absence of consistently tight construction, other musical features take on a heightened importance. Brahms wrote the sonata with Robert Hausmann, the cellist in Joseph Joachim's string quartet, in mind. Knowing Hausmann's complete mastery of the instrument, the composer asks a good deal more of the cellist and uses much more of the cello's range, especially in this first movement, than he had in op. 38. Other striking coloristic effects, in addition to extremes of register,

ing in *Free Composition*," *Music Theory Spectrum* 10 [1988]: 51). And see the evocative description of the effect of the retransition in James Webster, "The General and the Particular in Brahms's Later Sonata Forms," in *Brahms Studies*, 74–75.

27. Evans, *Handbook to the Music of Brahms*, 3:176.

include a good deal of surface chromaticism and the novel use of tremolos for both instruments.

Because Brahms revised the autograph of op. 99 so heavily, Geiringer
suggested that perhaps he "did not 'go for so many walks' with this work
as was otherwise his wont."[28] The first movement, in particular, contains
numerous revisions. An alternative explanation for the especially large
number of revisions here is that Brahms was experimenting with a new
kind of writing, not only in his use of sonata style, but also in the treatment of the cello-piano medium. Many of the revisions are very minor,
but the sheer number is surprising. Other, more substantial revisions
are clustered in and around the development and show the composer
carefully calculating the special effects that he creates in this part of
the movement. The loose design and eccentric style are most unusual,
yet the movement forms an effective foil to the highly developed slow
movement that follows. A contemporary critic probably had the two
first movements in mind when he observed that, although the second
sonata "is not at the same level as op. 38 with regard to thematic full
weight, it perhaps stands at yet a higher level with respect to formal
balance."[29]

* * *

Kalbeck's inspired idea offers an explanation for how Brahms may have
arrived at this balance within op. 99. In this instance, Kalbeck comes off
well altogether. Admittedly, the mystery surrounding Brahms's two cello
sonatas will not be fully solved until the autograph or engraver's model
of the original Adagio resurfaces. But a close study of the music and its
sources tends to support Kalbeck's intuition: the available evidence suggests that the slow movement of op. 99 might indeed derive from one
that had originally been destined for op. 38. And if the opening Allegro
vivace is the "most singular" movement of the later sonata, then the
Adagio affettuoso is surely, as Kalbeck would have it, the "soul" of the
work, its emotional and formal center of gravity.

28. Geiringer, 239.

29. [Adolf] Bernhard Vogel, in *Johannes Brahms: Sein Lebensgang und eine Würdigung seiner Werke*, vol. 4 of his *Musikheroen der Neuzeit* (Leipzig: Max Hesse, 1888), 38.

APPENDIX

Brahms's Chamber-Music Autographs

I have examined either the originals or the facsimiles of all extant autographs of Brahms's chamber pieces, with the exception of the String Quartet in B♭ Major, op. 67, and the Clarinet Sonatas in F Minor and E♭ Major, op. 120, that is, seventeen of twenty complete manuscripts: opp. 8 (first version), 18, 25, 26, 34, 36, 40, 51 (nos. 1 and 2), 78, 87, 88, 99, 101, 111, 114, and 115. (Partial autographs of opp. 60 and 100 are also extant; the whereabouts of the autographs of opp. 38 and 108, as well as the second version of op. 8 – assuming that there ever was a full separate autograph for it – are unknown.)

In the autographs of the late String Quintet in G Major, op. 111, the Clarinet Trio in A Minor, op. 114, and the Clarinet Quintet in B Minor, op. 115, Brahms seems to have used unfolded sheets of paper: the manufacturer's trademark appears on every other page of these autographs. Brahms, nevertheless, invariably has used any leftover systems on the final page of a movement to begin the following movement.

In fact, Brahms's habit in putting together his chamber-music manuscripts was consistent throughout his career. In the autograph of the first version of the Piano Trio in B Major, op. 8, he began the second movement directly after the first, even though only one system (of a possible three) remained on the reverse side of a sheet of paper; in the autograph of op. 115, the second movement also follows the first movement immediately on the reverse side of an apparently unfolded sheet of paper. The most extreme example of this habit occurs in the autograph of the String Quartet in C Minor, op. 51, no. 1, in which *each* of the succeeding movements directly follows the previous movement on the same page.

The only significant deviations from this practice that I have found in Brahms's chamber-music manuscripts, other than in the autograph of op. 99, occur in the autographs of the String Sextet in B♭ Major, op. 18, and the Violin Sonata in G Major, op. 78. Evidence in the correspondence suggests that Brahms may have sent off the first two movements of op. 78 before the Finale.[30] Brahms may have separated the first and fourth movements within the manuscript of op. 18 as well because he sent the Sextet to friends piecemeal. He sent only the first movement to Clara Schumann in November 1859; he clearly had sent the first three movements to Joachim before the Finale was complete.[31]

In the autographs of the Piano Quartet in A Major, op. 26 (at the end of the first movement), the Horn Trio in E♭ Major, op. 40 (at the end of the second and third movements), and the String Quartet in A Minor, op. 51, no. 2 (at the end of the second movement), Brahms did not use available space to begin the next movement, but he has not completely separated any individual movements within these autographs, as he did in op. 99 (and in opp. 18 and 78).

---

30. For an explanation of the separation of the Finale from the previous two movements in the autograph of op. 78, see Imogen Fellinger, "Brahms Sonate für Pianoforte und Violine op. 78: Ein Beitrag zum Schaffensprozeß des Meisters," *Musikforschung* 18 (1965): 16.

31. See *Schumann-Brahms Briefe*, 1:287; *Briefwechsel*, 5:284–85.

SIX

An Unwritten Metrical Modulation in Brahms's Intermezzo in E Minor, Op. 119, No. 2

Ira Braus

T he tempo markings in Johannes Brahms's Intermezzo in E Minor, op. 119, no. 2, raise a tantalizing interpretive question. The initial A section is headed *Andantino un poco agitato*; the middle B section, *Andantino grazioso*. Assuming that these markings signify contrasting tempos, should the pianist link the two sections proportionally, that is, by metrical modulation? To judge from several readings of the transition leading from A to B (ex. 6.1), performers have not typically done so.[1]

Gerhart Oppitz, for example, takes a *Luftpause* between the second and third beats of m. 35, suspending the tempo entirely; he then makes the third beat of m. 35 a discrete upbeat to the B section, whose tempo he gradually begins to accelerate. Julius Katchen takes a ritardando into m. 32, increases the tempo through mm. 32–34, and pauses on the half note of m. 35; he too treats the last beat of m. 35 as a discrete upbeat, but in his performance the ensuing Grazioso proceeds in an erratic tempo. Rudolf Serkin's reading resembles Katchen's, differing only in the establishment of the new tempo by m. 36. In contrast, Walter Klien executes the transition in tempo and then follows at a slightly brisker tempo starting with the upbeat to m. 36.

1. The performances sampled are by Gerhart Oppitz (Orfeo S020821A), Julius Katchen (London CM 9396), Rudolf Serkin (CBS Masterworks M 35177), and Walter Klien (VoxBox 431).

Example 6.1: Op. 119, no. 2, mm. 28–41.

In evaluating these performances, we must bear in mind that neither the autograph nor the first edition shows a fermata or ritardando during the transition. On the other hand, we would do well to remember that Brahms had once called for a simple metrical modulation of 2 : 1 to be introduced at the beginning of the B section; the autograph – although not the first edition – is marked *il doppio movimento* at m. 36.[2] The following analysis will propose that Brahms finally settled on linking the two sections by the more moderate proportion of 4 : 3, which he chose to notate in the published score only *implicitly*. As we shall discover, if this implied metrical modulation is tastefully executed, it not only enhances the graceful waltz character of the middle section but

2. This manuscript, which Brahms presented to Clara Schumann in June 1893, has been reproduced in facsimile as *Johannes Brahms: Intermezzi Opus 119, Nr. 2 und 3, Faksimile des Autographs*, with an afterword by Friedrich G. Zeileis (Tutzing: Hans Schneider, 1975). Other *Klavierstücke* in which Brahms explicitly called for sectional ritardandos and/or fermatas are op. 76, nos. 3 and 8, op. 116, nos. 2 and 6, op. 117, no. 3, and op. 118, nos. 2 and 5.

directs movement toward, within, and away from this passage more elegantly than does the metrically nonreferential rubato that is typically used.[3]

* * *

In her recent source study of the composer's late piano works, Camilla Cai has observed that Brahms "more than once reconsidered overall questions of tempo and character as they affect the balance and design of each piece." After recounting the composer's indecisiveness concerning the tempo marking for op. 119, no. 3, she notes, "Opus 119/2 shows similar changes already within the holograph. The more moderate 'Andantino un poco agitato' replaces 'Allegretto un poco agitato' for the opening tempo, yet the B section retains its ratio of 1 : 2. The engraver's copy omits that equivalency ratio, and balances instead 'Andantino un poco agitato' of the A section with a new marking, 'Andantino grazioso' for the B section. 'Andantino' for both sections suggests that there should be no significant tempo differences between them, only a character change."[4]

It is easy to understand why Brahms, having decided on a Grazioso character for the middle section, dispensed with the 2 : 1 ratio. Were the pianist to double the original tempo, the middle section would take on a *Schwung* better suited to the first movement of Schumann's *Faschingsschwank aus Wien* than to Brahms's graceful *Wiener Walzer*.[5] But that is

3. For a somewhat different view of the piece, see David Epstein, "Brahms and the Mechanisms of Musical Motion: The Composition of Performance," in *Brahms Studies*, 221–24. There can be no question, however, that Brahms was exploring the possibilities of the 4 : 3 proportion at the time the intermezzo was composed, during the early 1890s. Indeed, his most virtuosic uses of the relationship are evident in the nearly contemporaneous Sonatas for Clarinet and Piano, op. 120, although, to be sure, no modulation of tempo takes place. The opening movement of the first sonata contains a remarkable 4 : 3 proportional canon between the clarinet and the piano in mm. 183–86 that at once recalls fifteenth-century practice and anticipates ragtime music. This "ragtime element" appears also in the Finale of the second sonata (mm. 90–91, 141–43).

4. Camilla Kai, "Brahms's Short, Late Piano Pieces – Opus Numbers 116–119: A Source Study, an Analysis, and Performance Practice," 2 vols. (Ph.D. diss., Boston University, 1986), 1:75–76. See also her "Was Brahms a Reliable Editor? Changes Made in Opuses 116, 117, 118, and 119," *Acta musicologica* 61 (1989): 83–101.

5. Curiously, Ilona Eibenschütz, who gave the first public performance of op. 119, no. 2 (see McCorkle, 475), apparently did play the B section at very nearly *doppio movimento*. One of her performances of the piece has been preserved on the recording *Pupils of Clara Schumann* (Pearl CLA1000).

not to say that the B section should be played *lo stesso tempo*. On the contrary, I would argue that a small but significant tempo change goes a long way toward highlighting the characteristic difference between an Un poco agitato (A) and a Grazioso (B). We might begin to explore this hypothesis by examining the thematic structure of the piece.

The intermezzo is essentially monothematic (ex. 6.2). The A theme is declaimed anapestically (♫♪ ♫♪) and supported by a rhythmic "half canon" (the left hand's expected eighth note is actually an eighth-note rest); the B theme, in the parallel major, is declaimed cretically (♩.♪♩) and supported by arpeggios. These differences have important implications for the tempo. To project the A section's tune-cum-canon – and, more important, its offbeat slurring – the player must feel a quarter-note rather than a dotted-half-note impulse; otherwise, the music gallops away, *molto agitato*. If the B section were to be played at the same tempo as the A section, the resulting pace of three beats to the measure might well split the melody up into one-measure modules, thereby disrupting the music's underlying *Vierhebigkeit*. At the same time, such a reading of the B section would tend to suppress an implied offbeat phrasing that is borrowed from A (see ex. 6.2). Just as in m. 1 the soprano G "belongs" to B rather than to the preceding C, so in m. 36 the G♯ belongs to B rather than to C♯. A small increase in the tempo would help project this parallel; the faster tempo would more equitably distribute the measure's center of accentual gravity (from the first beat), so that, in a reworking of the A section's offbeat phrasing, the eighth-note rests would "rise" to the third beat rather than "fall" from the first. The faster tempo would produce a one-to-the-measure impulse, which would emphasize the third beat's motion over the bar line. It would increase the tempo just enough, that is, to project the B section's easy *Vierhebigkeit*, creating a foil to the A section's turbulent, asymmetrical diction.[6]

The advantages of taking a somewhat faster tempo for the Grazioso raise some practical problems. How should the two tempos be related proportionally? Where should the change be implemented? As we have seen, Brahms dropped his original plan simply to double the tempo at the outset of the B section. What we are left with is notation that implies instead a more seamless (and striking) change occurring well before

6. Perhaps the most cogent reason for feeling the B section in one can be found in mm. 52–54, where the *Vierhebigkeit* decomposes into nothing less than 2 + 2.

Example 6.2: Op. 119, no. 2: *a*, mm. 1–2; *b*, mm. 36–39.

the double bar (see ex. 6.1). In mm. 29–31, the left hand plays arpeggios that articulate groups of three sixteenth notes. Brahms highlights two of these groups by double-stemming and dotting the first note, thereby marking dotted-eighth-note impulses; the other groups emerge naturally out of registral disjunction. Following the suggestion of this notation, the performer can modulate to a new tempo that is approximately 25 percent faster than the prevailing one if (1) the emergent dotted eighth note becomes the new quarter note and (2) the resulting 4 : 3 proportion is introduced on the downbeat of m. 32.[7]

Significantly, this proposed metrical modulation is relevant to the broad tonal moves of the piece, from the E minor of the Un poco agitato to the E major of the Grazioso (and back again). As shown in ex. 6.1, the passage leading to the B section is marked by three appearances of a pitch cell embracing both $\sharp\hat{3}$ and $\natural\hat{3}$ (G♯–G♮–F♯). Unobtrusively introduced in an inner voice in m. 32, this cell becomes prominent in mm. 33–34 as a half-note hemiola configuration while being echoed "heterophonically" in the accompaniment.[8] If the prevailing tempo is increased by 25 percent during this passage, then the cell will continue to work anacrusically through the hemiola, as it had done in the preceding measure. This "passing" augmentation stretches the structural up-

7. I would suggest metronome markings for A and B (from m. 32) of ♩ = ca. 72 and ♩ = ca. 90, respectively. How might a performer learn to track the dotted-eighth-note impulse in mm. 29–31 prior to its becoming the new quarter note? I advise this strategy. Practice the left hand alone, counting the large beats aloud and playing only the first notes of each dotted-eighth-note group through m. 32. (The task may be hard at first since the dotted eighth notes elude the "normal" 4 : 3 partitioning of the $\frac{3}{4}$ measure, with articulations on the first, fourth, seventh, and tenth sixteenth notes). Repeat until the metrical modulation becomes ingrained. Then play the transition *come scritto.*

8. As David Lewin observed to me in a personal communication, this chromatic cell is anticipated in mm. 4–5 (E–E♭–D) and m. 17 (A–A♭–G). The cell's final precursor appears in mm. 28–29 (C–B–A♯–A–A♭).

beat starting in the middle of the first beat of m. 32 beyond the hemiola to the next, more significant structural downbeat, in m. 36. With this lessening of the hemiola's inherent ritardando effect, the move from minor to major does indeed become transitional: rather than prematurely closing the A section on a chimerical *tierce de Picardie*, $\sharp\hat{3}$ gradually opens up the B section. In a well-executed 4 : 3 modulation, the first downbeat of the Grazioso hovers between repose and motion, as if the initial waltz step barely touched the ground.

Introducing the change in tempo as I have suggested would have several additional advantages. In many performances, the music grinds unfortunately to a halt on the A–C dyad at the end of m. 31. This dyad does mark the pitch climax of mm. 29–32, to be sure, but its weak metrical position and lack of lower-voice support make it an unlikely point of arrival. In a performance using the 4 : 3 modulation, however, the A–C dyad would propel the phrase that had begun in m. 29 directly into the first beat of m. 32, with the alto line swooping down to the B in the tenor. The tonic chord on the downbeat of m. 32, itself lacking textural completion, would in turn initiate motion to a point of greater tension, the suspension chain commencing in m. 33 and culminating two measures later in V^7 harmony. Meanwhile, the soprano's D$\sharp$ and A$\sharp$ in m. 32 would be projected with greater contrapuntal integrity than otherwise would be the case, as foreground events (incomplete neighbor tones) rather than middleground events (agents in the tonicization of the soprano's $\hat{1}$ and $\hat{5}$). In short, the 4 : 3 modulation would direct our attention to the goal of the section – the major inflection in m. 32 – rather than to its initiation.

The emphasis on m. 32 is important since a long-range motivic process is completed there involving the ascending leap of the octave in the bass (ex. 6.3). As first presented, in m. 14, the octave begins on beat 3 and lasts less than a single beat; in m. 22, it begins on the second beat and continues to the third; finally, in m. 32, it is initiated on the downbeat and embraces the entire measure. (And how beautifully the motive expands through an additional octave at the climax of the B section, in m. 63!) Yet to retain the prevailing tempo at m. 32 would be to overemphasize the structural importance of the upper Es and, retrospectively, the lower one, too, by unduly stressing the pitch as a harmonic point of arrival. The E on the second and third beats – already contained within the low E on the downbeat as its brighter second partial – prefigures the color shift from minor to major. In other words, the

Example 6.3: Op. 119, no. 2: *a*, m. 14; *b*, m. 22; *c*, m. 32.

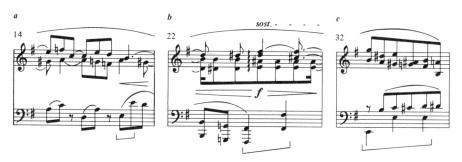

modulation of timbre is an emergent property of not only harmonic but also tempo modulation.

The proposed 4 : 3 modulation would also enhance perception of the crucial G♯–G♮–F♯ pitch cell in m. 32 and its quadruple augmentation in mm. 33–34. The resulting one-to-the-measure impulse, at once establishing the new tempo of B and linking the Un poco agitato to the Grazioso, would keep the latter's waltz character in *Takt*. In this reading, then, the tempo of m. 35 would remain constant throughout, rather than decomposing, as generally occurs, into one tempo for the first two beats and another for the third beat and following. Obviously, a mechanical performance of m. 35 is not desirable, but if any rubato is to be applied, it ought to occur within a single tempo.

A similar metrical modulation would make for a felicitous return to the reprise (ex. 6.4). One need only imagine the double-eighth-note pickup in m. 71 as two dotted sixteenth notes in the A tempo, keeping the thirty-second note as the least common submultiple and thereby expressing the 4:3 on the next smaller scale of duration. Especially telling in this passage are Brahms's tempo markings: *tempo primo* is entered *after* the indications *poco rit. - - - - in tempo*.

Finally, the original 4 : 3 modulation should be reintroduced in m. 96, by analogy to m. 32, and the resultant faster tempo maintained through the ensuing coda (ex. 6.5). In these final measures, Brahms does more than allude to the B section; at the very end, he also recalls the hemiola that had originally led to that section. Diminution and augmentation again are integrated, but now in a new way: in m. 103, an "inverted" hemiola in the left hand (reinforcing the $\frac{6}{8}$ division that is implied already by the alto and tenor in the previous measure) supports a real (albeit incomplete) hemiola in the right hand ($\frac{3}{2}$). Here, in the left hand's concluding arpeggio, Brahms actually comes his closest to artic-

Example 6.4: Op. 119, no. 2, mm. 67b–74.

ulating the "normal" disposition of a $4:3$ division within the $\frac{3}{4}$ measure; the suggested change in tempo would make this structure cognizable.

* * *

The use of the $4:3$ modulation would thus link the intermezzo's structural divisions by relating its pitch, temporal, and even timbral domains. It would emphasize Brahms's monothematicism while giving fresh insight into his subtle art of transition. And it would offer performers an alternative to the rhythmic guesswork, whether inspired or not, that seems to characterize execution of the transitions. But a problem remains, of course. With all these apparent advantages, we are left to wonder why the composer was satisfied merely to hint at the crucial modulation in his notation. Perhaps he thought that his contemporaries would have balked at a metrical modulation more complicated than $1:n$.[9] But what if the intermezzo had been composed in 1950? In that circumstance, might not Brahms have explicitly notated the metrical modulation in his score?

9. To be sure, toward the end of the Second Piano Concerto, Brahms did call for a $4:3$ modulation, but he indicated this through his metronome markings, not an equation. The modulation is quite straightforward, inasmuch as a repeated pattern of three sixteenth notes in the old tempo is carried over into the new faster tempo as a pattern of eighth-note triplets (see David Epstein, *Beyond Orpheus* [Cambridge, Mass.: MIT Press, 1979], 94–95, and "Brahms and the Mechanisms of Musical Motion," 206–11).

SEVEN

Brahms on Schopenhauer:
The *Vier ernste Gesänge*, Op. 121, and Late Nineteenth-Century Pessimism

Daniel Beller-McKenna

In his essay on Brahms and the Bible, Martin Meiser questions whether the composer would have chosen the same "God-trusting" (*Gottvertrauende*) texts for his *Deutsches Requiem* (1868) had he written the piece at the end rather than during the middle of his life. Meiser contends that the late *Vier ernste Gesänge* (1896), settings of four biblical texts, argue against such a conclusion and adds, "Perhaps we have to account for a development toward greater skepticism, comparable to that of Ecclesiastes."[1] This conclusion may be warranted if one limits one's view to the texts of op. 121, nos. 1 and 2 (Eccles. 3:19–22 and 4:1–3, respectively), words that are far more pessimistic than anything to be found in the *Requiem*. Even the consoling image of death offered by the third song, "O Tod" (Ecclus. 41:1–4), is less comforting than the image of death in the earlier work.

But Meiser's pessimistic assessment of the *Serious Songs* – one shared by many – ignores the positive message of no. 4, in which Brahms sets Paul's hymn on love from 1 Cor. 13. A pessimistic view must treat the set as an unintegrated and imbalanced whole in which the fourth song stands alone, out of kilter with the consistently gloomy message of the first three. Not surprisingly, the last song has widely been held in lesser opinion than the others. Eric Sams, for example, remarks that "the last

---

1. Martin Meiser, "Brahms und die Bibel," *Musik und Kirche* 53 (1983): 295. Unless otherwise noted, all translations are my own.

(fine though it is) is usually thought to be the least compelling. Unlike the first three, it lacks the sense of being the definitive expression of its text." To Michael Musgrave the "music seems to fit this text with less of a sense of inevitability than in the other settings," while Malcolm Boyd states flatly that "it really has no place in this cycle."[2]

Of course not all critics have shared this opinion. Some have accepted no. 4 as a message of hopefulness amid the despair of life. Yet even those who embrace the fourth song tend to reject an ultimately optimistic message in the whole cycle. Instead, they find the crux of the set closer to the middle, particularly in no. 3 ("O Tod"), as if the Corinthians text were a mere afterthought, intended to soften the heavy blow of the first three songs. According to such a view, the praise of the dead expressed in no. 2 ("So I praised the dead more than the living") is developed by the focus on death in no. 3, with the whole cycle forming what Karl Geiringer calls "an overwhelming Hymn to Death."[3]

To understand the *Vier ernste Gesänge* in this way, however, misses the point. Indeed, this essay will develop the argument that the optimism of the last song is not a direct reaction to the death imagery of the third but rather addresses the pessimism expressed in the first two – a pessimism that goes far beyond death to the bleak statement in the middle of the second song that the one who is not yet born is better than the dead and the living. More specifically, Brahms's choice, placement, and musical settings of texts in op. 121 will be read as his encounter with a dominant philosophical trend of the age (Schopenhauer's pessimism) and ultimate rejection of that trend in favor of an earlier stance (Romantic Idealism).

I

"Vanity of vanities! All is vanity," Ecclesiastes begins. Qoheleth, as the author is called in the original Hebrew, presents a basic philosophy in the opening chapter, concluding, "It is an unhappy business that God has given to human beings to be busy with. I saw all the deeds that are done under the sun; and see, all is vanity and a chasing after wind" (Eccles. 1:13–14).[4]

2. Eric Sams, *Brahms Songs* (London: British Broadcasting Corp., 1972), 64; Musgrave, 266; Malcolm Boyd, "Brahms and the Four Serious Songs," *Musical Times* 107 (1967): 593.

3. Geiringer, 287.

4. For the most part, biblical passages are provided in English as found in *The New Oxford Annotated Bible* (New Revised Standard Version), ed. Bruce M. Metzger and Roland E. Murphy

The texts that Brahms chose for his first two songs – Eccles. 3:19–22 and 4:1–3, respectively – use death as a focal point from which to examine a number of the opening chapter's premises:

> Denn es gehet dem Menschen wie dem Vieh, wie dies stirbt, so stirbt er auch; und haben alle einerlei Odem; und der Mensch hat nichts mehr denn das Vieh: denn es ist alles eitel. Es fährt alles an einen Ort; es ist alles von Staub gemacht, und wird wieder zu Staub. Wer weiss, ob der Geist des Menschen aufwärts fahre, und der Odem des Viehes unterwärts unter die Erde fahre? Darum sahe ich, dass nichts bessers ist, denn das der Mensch fröhlich sei in seiner Arbeit; denn das ist sein Teil. Denn wer will ihn dahin bringen, dass er sehe, was nach ihm geschehen wird?

> (For the fate of humans and the fate of animals is the same; as one dies, so dies the other. They all have the same breath and humans have no advantage over the animals; for all is vanity. All go to one place; all are from the dust, and all turn to dust again. Who knows whether the human spirit goes upward and the spirit of animals goes downward to the earth? So I saw that there is nothing better than that all should enjoy their work, for that is their lot; who can bring them to see what will be after them?)

> Ich wandte mich, und sahe an alle, die Unrecht leiden unter der Sonne; und siehe, da waren Tränen derer, die Unrecht litten und hatten keinen Tröster, und die ihnen Unrecht Täten, waren zu mächtig, dass sie keinen Tröster haben konnten. Da lobte ich die Toten, die schon gestorben waren, mehr als die Lebendigen, die noch das Leben hatten; Und der noch nicht ist, ist besser als alle beide, und des Bösen nicht inne wird, das unter der Sonne geschieht.

> (*I turned and* saw all the oppressions that are practiced under the sun. Look, the tears of the oppressed – with no one to comfort them! On the side of their oppressors there was power – with no one to comfort them. And I thought the dead, who have already died, more fortunate than the living, who are still alive; but better than both is the one who has not yet been, and has not seen the evil deeds that are done under the sun.)

Death is the fate that awaits human beings just as it awaits beasts. Our knowledge of death is futile, as is our toil: "All is vanity and a chasing after wind." But the most powerful and nihilistic message in the two

(New York: Oxford University Press, 1991). Where the Lutheran text used by Brahms in op. 121 differs significantly from the newer English version, however, I have provided my own translation, as indicated by italicized text.

texts is sounded at the end of the second: the dead are better off than the living, but not as fortunate as those who have not yet been born.

That extreme pessimism most immediately calls to mind the philosophy of Arthur Schopenhauer. His philosophy of the "Will," written in the first quarter of the nineteenth century but not popular until after 1850, constitutes a negative reaction to the metaphysical flights of two early nineteenth-century contemporaries, Fichte's Ego and Hegel's World Spirit. Rather than secularizing the God of Christianity by placing him within ourselves and nature, as the Romantics had, Schopenhauer eliminated the spiritual element. He replaced an all-knowing or progressive force with the blind and undirected Will; there is no guiding hand, no plan, no God. Such a state of affairs renders our empirical actions and contemplations meaningless, or at least pointless; hence the great sense of pessimism in Schopenhauer's philosophy.

Brahms first became aware of Schopenhauer's thought as it appeared in *Parerga und Paralipomena,* a somewhat distilled and popularized version of the ideas from the philosopher's magnum opus, *The World as Will and Representation* (henceforth *WWR*).[5] Max Kalbeck tells of how Brahms became familiar with *Parerga und Paralipomena* early on through his association with the pianist Carl Tausig in 1862. According to Kalbeck, Tausig had long discussions with Brahms in which he tried to win the composer over to the philosophy of *WWR.* In the end, Tausig was unsuccessful; Brahms, Kalbeck noted, had already "had enough with the 'Parerga.' "[6]

Whatever he might have thought of Schopenhauer, it is difficult to believe that Brahms did not have the philosopher in mind when he began work on the *Vier ernste Gesänge.* Kalbeck, who was Brahms's close friend as well as biographer, points out that "the famous and notorious ch. 46 of the supplemental second volume to Schopenhauer's main work, *The World as Will and Representation,* shows the influence of 'Pre-

5. Arthur Schopenhauer, *Parerga and Paralipomena,* 2 vols., trans. E. F. J. Payne (Oxford: Clarendon Press, 1974), and *The World as Will and Representation,* 2 vols., trans. E. F. J. Payne (New York: Dover, 1966).

6. Kalbeck, *Brahms,* 2:37–38. Tausig's failure notwithstanding, Brahms did acquire a copy of *WWR* at some point. The book remained in his library at his death and included "copious marginal notes" (see Hofmann, 104). Moreover, Brahms preserved a letter in Schopenhauer's hand in his autograph collection, which consisted primarily of scores and letters from artists whom Brahms admired or at least respected (see Kalbeck, *Brahms,* 4:232–33).

diger Salomo' [the Lutheran title for Ecclesiastes]."[7] More important, several images and figures from this chapter, entitled "On the Vanity and Suffering of Life," recall Brahms's chosen texts. A pair of quotations near the end of the chapter draws an especially close connection to the pessimistic ending of the second song. A passage from Plutarch, "Pity him who is born, because he faces so many evils; but the dead are to be accompanied with mirth and blessings because they have escaped from so many sufferings," is followed by one from Plato's *Apology of Socrates*, "Not to be born would be the best thing for man, never to behold the sun's scorching rays; but if one is born, then one is to press as quickly as possible to the portals of Hades, and rest there under the earth" (*WWR*, 2:586). Both passages resonate with Ecclesiastes. Schopenhauer's citations, therefore, suggest the fairly direct influence of that biblical text on the philosopher.

Schopenhauer's skepticism must have been anathema to Brahms. Not one to be accused of blind optimism and faith, Brahms nevertheless accepted the traditional Lutheran culture of his native North Germany and maintained a strong sense of spirituality, whether or not that translated into concrete religious beliefs. He had already expressed his spiritual acceptance of death in such works as the *Requiem* and the motet "Warum ist das Licht gegeben?" op. 74, no. 1, in which an initial inability to come to grips with death is progressively replaced by an understanding of death as "selig" or "sanft und stille." Moreover, Brahms's dark side was colored in Romantic *Sehnsucht* and melancholy, not in the vanity and despair expressed by Schopenhauer. And, as we shall see, that dark side never completely overshadowed the sense of hope and progress engendered by the idealist philosophies of the first half of the century.

II

Given his identification with the more spiritual and forward-looking elements of Romanticism, it may seem ironic that Brahms chose for his first two songs texts that fit so well with Schopenhauer's pessimistic philosophy. But rather than concluding, with Meiser and others, that Brahms's choices here reflected his own "development toward greater skepticism," we can best understand the situation if we consider them against the text with which he chose to end his cycle: 1 Cor. 13:1–3, 12–13. That text is especially optimistic and un-Schopenhauerian:

7. Kalbeck, *Brahms*, 4:455.

Wenn ich mit Menschen- und mit Engelzungen redete, und hätte der Liebe nicht, so wär' ich ein tönend Erz, oder eine klingende Schelle. Und wenn ich weissagen könnte und wüsste alle Geheimnisse und alle Erkenntnis, und hätte allen Glauben, also, dass ich Berge versetzte; und hätte der Liebe nicht, so wäre ich nichts. Und wenn ich alle meine Habe den Armen gäbe, und liesse meinen Leib brennen; und hätte der Liebe nicht, so wäre mirs nichts nütze. . . . Wir sehen jetzt durch einen Spiegel in einem dunkeln Worte, dann aber von Angesicht zu Angesichte. Jetzt erkenne ichs stückweise, dann aber werd ichs erkennen, gleich wie ich erkenet bin. Nun aber bleibet Glaube, Hoffnung, Liebe, diese drei; aber die Liebe ist die grösseste unter ihnen.

(If I speak in the tongues of mortals and of angels, but do not have love, I am a noisy gong or a clanging cymbal. And if I have prophetic powers, and understand all mysteries and all knowledge, and if I have all faith, so as to remove mountains, but do not have love, I am nothing. If I give away all my possessions, and if I hand over my body so that I may boast, but do not have love, I gain nothing. . . . For now we see in a mirror as *in a dark word*, but then we will see face to face. Now I know only in part, then I will know fully, even as I have been fully known. And now faith hope and love abide, these three; and the greatest of these is love.)

The philosophy expressed in this text would certainly have echoed Brahms's Romantic affinities, for in many ways – as I will argue – it can be read as an early nineteenth-century German Romantic manifesto on love.

Verses 1–11 are filled with familiar biblical concepts: wisdom, prophecy, faith, and hope. Each is found lacking when compared to love, which is the "greatest of these." Standing conspicuously outside the typical biblical imagery in this text, however, is the mirror metaphor. It appears as the second of three "now-then" completions in vv. 11 (which Brahms omitted) and 12:

1. When I was a child, I spoke like a child, I thought like a child, I reasoned like a child; when I became an adult, I put an end to childish ways.

2. For now we see in a mirror, dimly, but then we will see face to face.

3. Now I know only in part; then I will know fully, even as I have been fully known.

In this context, seeing in a mirror is equivalent to "speaking, thinking, and reasoning like a child," or "knowing only in part"; that is, it reveals only a portion of what will later be revealed "face to face." According to its position within the completion group, the mirror acts as a medium between the purely human experience of completion (maturity from childhood to adulthood) and the spiritual experience of completion (knowing fully). It brings us toward being "face to face" with the divine and thus provides a transitional stage toward coming to know the divine. The overall sense of completion in vv. 11–12 also suggests a Hegelian synthesis in which a state of mortal incompleteness not only is fulfilled but brings one to a new level of being, a new unity. That synthesis is brought about by love.[8]

Removed from a Christian context (made all the easier by the lack of any reference to God, Christ, or anything specifically Judeo-Christian), 1 Cor. 13 contains the elements for some important philosophies of love in the Romantic age, most notably those of Georg Wilhelm Friedrich Hegel and Friedrich Hölderlin. Hegel and Hölderlin were fellow students at the Lutheran Theological Seminary in Tübingen from 1788 to 1793 and were therefore surely familiar with Paul's epistles. Divinity and love are closely intertwined and appear in strikingly Pauline language in Hegel's earliest statement on love:

> Where subject and object [read "mortal" and "image of the mortal"] . . . are thought as united . . . [they] are not to be separated – such an ideal is the object of every religion. Divinity is at once subject and object, one [can]not say of it that it is subject in opposition to object or that it has an object – . . . only in love alone is one at one with the object. . . . This love, made by the imagination into an entity, is the divinity. . . . Love can only take place against its equal, against the mirror, against the echo of our existence. . . . Religion is one with love. The beloved is not opposed to us, he is one with our essential being, we see only ourselves in him – and yet also he is still not we – a miracle that we cannot grasp.[9]

Love, which is "the divinity," can take place only when we recognize ourselves in the object, "against the mirror, against the echo of our existence." And it is in this divinity that we recognize ourselves, but "cannot grasp" the miracle that "he is still not we," and so we see only "dimly."

8. Paul W. Gooch provides a more thorough discussion of the mirror as a completion metaphor in *Partial Knowledge: Philosophical Studies in Paul* (Notre Dame, Ind.: University of Notre Dame Press, 1987), 142–62, esp. 147–51.

9. G. W. F. Hegel, "Two Fragments of 1797 on Love," trans. H. S. Harris and Cyrus Hamlin, *Clio* 8 (1987): 261–62.

The references to opposition and the mirror in Hegel's writing point to the important role that Hölderlin's thought played in his development around this time. Hölderlin focuses on the opposition brought about by difference, especially the opposition of "love" and "selfhood." "In regard to the opposition of these two," writes Dieter Henrich, "unification takes on an entirely new function with Hölderlin: no longer bound together are . . . person and person, but tendencies of life, of which one is itself union. Love thus becomes the metaprinciple for the unification of opposites in man."[10] When Hölderlin's unifying power is added to those qualities of love expressed by Hegel, Paul's influence on Romantic theories of love seems overwhelming.

Such an affinity could hardly have been overlooked by Brahms, steeped as he was in Romantic literature and ideology, on the one hand, and in the Bible, on the other. His selection of Paul's text to complete a cycle begun by the pessimistic Qoheleth creates a direct confrontation between antagonistic philosophies: the Schopenhauerian pessimism expressed in the first two songs contrasts strongly with the Romantic spirituality promoted in the last.

The text of no. 3 (Ecclus. 41:1–4) provides the necessary transition. It is drawn from the apocryphal Ecclesiasticus, or the Wisdom of Jesus the Son of Sirach, which, like Ecclesiastes, dates from the second century B.C. Sirach, however, offers a far more traditional and religious outlook on life and death, "as if Job and Ecclesiastes had never been written":[11]

> O Tod, wie bitter bist du, wenn an dich gedenket ein Mensch, der gute Tage und genug hat und ohne Sorge lebet, und dem es wohl geht in allen Dingen und noch wohl essen mag! O Tod, wie wohl tust du dem Dürftigen, der da schwach und alt ist, der in allen Sorgen steckt, und nichts Bessers zu hoffen, noch zu erwarten hat!

> (O death, how bitter is the thought of you to the one at peace among possessions, who has nothing to worry about and is prosperous in everything, and still is vigorous enough to enjoy food! O death how *sweet you are* to one who is *old* and failing in strength, worn down by age, *and has nothing better to hope for or expect!*)

---

10. Dieter Henrich, "Hegel and Hölderlin," *Idealistic Studies* 2 (1972): 156.

11. Bruce M. Metzger and Roland E. Murphy, introduction to "Ecclesiasticus, or the Wisdom of Jesus Son of Sirach," in *The New Oxford Annotated Bible*, AP 86.

The healthy man in the first half of the text sees death as bitter, while the old and sick man in the second half welcomes it. Death here is no longer the great equalizer of Ecclesiastes but something closer to the traditional comforter of Lutheran thought. By focusing on death, Sirach already offers a major step toward a more spiritual attitude than that manifested in the texts of the first two songs. Significantly, Sirach presents death as a much more palatable choice than nonexistence, in stark contrast to the preferences espoused by Qoheleth (and Schopenhauer). Death is able to serve a mediating function in op. 121 for two reasons: because it is inherently balanced in the Sirach text and because that balance renders it less extreme than the nihilistic outlook of Qoheleth. Brahms's choice and placement of the Sirach text, therefore, enhances the powerful impact of Qoheleth's claim that nonexistence is preferable to life or death by posing a more acceptable foil against it.

III

Brahms discussed op. 121 at length with Kalbeck and Gustav Ophüls.[12] Perhaps it was his own tendency to discuss the songs as a group that has led to an ongoing perception that they form an indivisible unit – a cycle. And the expectations that a listener would bring to a cycle might, in turn, account for the previously discussed problems in the reception of no. 4. Indeed, nos. 1–3 seem to follow smoothly from one another harmonically and even share common melodic motifs (ex. 7.1). Not only is the set marked by a tonally progressive key scheme, passing from D minor to G minor/major to E minor/major by the end of no. 3, but, in addition, the end of each song is motivically connected to the beginning of the next. By contrast, there is apparently no similar logic in the shift from E major to E♭ major between nos. 3 and 4 nor any obvious motivic connections between them comparable to those linking the first three songs.

The failure to perceive a musical relation between the fourth song and what precedes it goes hand in hand with the notion that the musical progression from the beginning of no. 1 to the end of no. 3 is continuous and unbroken. In fact, it is not. Just as a death-centered view of the texts to the first three songs overlooks the nihilistic depths of no. 2, so does an interpretation of nos. 1–3 as a seamless musical whole ignore

12. See Kalbeck, *Brahms*, 4:432–34, 437–44; and Gustav Ophüls, *Erinnerungen an Johannes Brahms* (Berlin: Verlag der Deutschen Brahms-Gesellschaft, 1921), 25–30, 40–45.

Example 7.1: Op. 121, nos. 1–3: harmonic and motivic connections between songs.

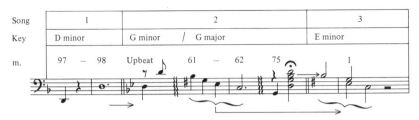

the wrenching turn of harmony and interruption to which those depths are set (no. 2, mm. 52–61), an interruption that brings the music out of the D/G minor realm and into the sharp-side keys of E minor and E major. While presenting Qoheleth's darkest utterance, Brahms interjects a profound moment of silence (m. 55). The subsequent move to the notes A♯–B and the cadence in E minor that follows (mm. 57–61) mark a pivotal moment in the cycle.

In fact, B♮ is the critical note on which the *Serious Songs* turn. Dramatically introduced in both parts in m. 57, where it sounds as $\hat{5}$ in E minor, it permeates the entire closing section of the song. Not only is it the last note sung in no. 2 (now sounding as $\hat{3}$ in G major), but it is the first sounded in no. 3, where it is heard again as $\hat{5}$ in E minor. Significantly, no. 3 is the only song in which the voice enters before the piano or with the pitch it had last sung in the previous song. To appreciate the disruptive effect brought on by the B♮ introduced in m. 57, we must consider how smoothly the first two songs lead up to that moment.

Death is indeed a central theme through the entire first song and the first half of the second. The text of no. 1 presents death as the great equalizer of men and beasts and concludes that we should be happy in our work, for there is nothing to be taken with us from this life. In no. 2 the text "turns" (*wendet sich*) from thoughts of death to examine life, finding it full of evil and lacking consolation. Not only does death negate the advantages that we thought we held in life (the message of the previous song), but life itself, we are now told, is not worth living in the first place. These thoughts lead logically to the conclusion that the unborn are better than the dead or the living.

Brahms's setting to this point reflects the sense of the texts sympathetically. In no. 1, for example, the sentiment that we should be happy in our work is posed in the form of a question ("Who can bring them to see what will be after them?"), thereby diminishing the formal closure of the song's text.[13] At first glance, no. 1 would seem to be the most harmonically closed of the four, the only one to begin and end in and on its tonic harmony (D minor). But a closer look reveals a fundamental instability of the tonic key throughout the song, which is due to the nearly constant pedal on the dominant (A). By persisting so relentlessly, that pedal undermines the tonic identity of the prevailing D-minor harmony, and it provides an unsettling "question" that requires resolution in the form of a tonic "answer." Example 7.2 traces the melodic path of the tonic pedal that eventually arrives in the closing section (mm. 82–98). There, while the D pedal provides closure at a deep structural level (aptly reflected by the extremely deep register of the piano's left hand), it fails to provide resolution on the surface because it is unable to free itself there from the dominant pitch. In mm. 92–94,

Example 7.2: Melodic path of tonic pedals in op. 121, no. 1, mm. 82–96.

for example, a pedal on A remains in the right hand of the piano, undercutting the V–I motion in the bass. At the same time, the voice focuses on the same note, leaving the rhetorical question "Denn wer will ihn dahin bringen, dass er sehe, was nach ihm geschehen wird?" melodically unanswered as well. Finally, the plagal cadence in mm. 95–96 leaves the song without a final V–I cadence, diminishing the sense of closure at the harmonic level.

Even the forceful D-minor chords that end no. 1 (ex. 7.3*a*) fail to provide a firm tonic conclusion. They directly recall the earlier question in the song, "Wer weiss ob der Geist des Menschen aufwärts fahre?" where the same falling and rising octaves on D initiated a pair of conflicting arpeggios: one rising through B♭ major in the voice, another descending through G minor in the left hand of the accompaniment (ex. 7.3*b*). Thus the final D-minor chords recall a *musically* ambiguous

13. In his notebook of biblical texts, in which all the texts to op. 121 appear (Vienna, Stadt-und Landesbibliothek, HIN 55.733), Brahms added an editorial exclamation point in parentheses after the phrase "fröhlich sein in seiner Arbeit." It is difficult to say with certainty what Brahms meant by this, but quite likely the annotation was intended to be an ironic comment on Qoheleth's words.

Example 7.3: Octave leaps in op. 121, no. 1: *a*, mm. 97–98;
b, mm. 45–49.

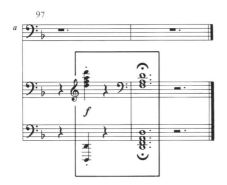

moment in the song while they reinforce the *textual* lack of closure by recalling an earlier question.

This oblique allusion at the end of no. 1 to a descending G-minor arpeggio (D–B♭–G–D) also provides a transition into no. 2, which begins with the same figure, now as a tonic harmony. In this way, the first half of the second song unfolds directly out of no. 1. Brahms subjects the G-minor arpeggio to a series of transmutations in mm. 1–35 that can all be categorized as "descending figures" (ex. 7.4) and that, as a group, are generally extended downward through the next twenty measures. The original arpeggio (ex. 7.4*a*) begins dissolving into a chain of descending thirds at m. 7 (ex. 7.4*b*), before re-forming as a descending E♭-major arpeggio in m. 16 (ex. 7.4*c*). Like the text, which delves further into the lot of "all who suffer injustice under the sun," the music of this section probes the tonic key by touching on related key areas: E♭ major, C minor, G major. Finally, the most distant mutation of the descending figure (mm. 27–28) reaches down the octave below the song's opening notes (ex. 7.4*e*).

Example 7.4: Descending figures in op. 121, no. 2: *a*, mm. 1–2;
b, mm. 7–8; *c*, mm. 19–20; *d*, mm. 23–24; *e*, mm. 27–28.

At m. 36, Qoheleth passes judgment on all that he has seen in mm. 1–35. Brahms begins his setting of each textual phrase here with the familiar descending figures, creating an increasing sense of concentration, which leads up to the crucial turning point at mm. 55–57. The voice joins the range of the accompanimental bass line with a *pianissimo* diminished-seventh arpeggio (C–A–F♯–D♯–C) at the words "Und der noch nicht ist" (mm. 52–54), heightening the tension before the song comes to a complete standstill in m. 55. It is not the A♯ of m. 56 – which sounds at first like a B♭ in the tonic key – but the move to B♮ in m. 57 that drives home the impact of the text that follows: the one who does not yet exist "ist besser als alle beide." Textually, this is the darkest moment in the cycle; musically, it is one of the quietest and yet most powerful. Brahms places the critical move away from G minor at the most radical, the most "Schopenhauerian" line of text among the four songs. Both the note B and the E-minor harmony of m. 57 point ahead to G major (mm. 61–75) and to E minor (no. 3). And, when in mm. 60–61 the voice rises an octave to begin the last section of the song, it joins with the accompanimental bass once more, precisely as the piano initiates the descending series of thirds (B–G–E–C–A–F♯) that later will begin no. 3.

Everything, then, points outward and away from what has led up to m. 57. In his analysis of op. 121, Arnold Whittall writes that "the appropriateness of the major-key resolution [to no. 2] may . . . be questioned

{182}

in view of the nature of the text."[14] Indeed, G major seems a puzzling key in which to end the song if we assume that the music is *reflecting* the text. If, however, we understand the music to be *commenting* on the text, to be *reacting* to it, then the musical move away from what has come before makes sense. It is not, after all, Qoheleth who provides the striking musical setting to his dismal conclusions, but Brahms. To continue in the same musical direction – by remaining in G minor or, perhaps, by returning to the key of D minor – would be to follow the meaning of the text. But Brahms, or the musical persona that he creates in these songs, chooses not to follow Qoheleth into the darkness. In my view, Brahms is reacting less to what the closing thought of no. 2 stands for within Ecclesiastes than to its close congruence with the most radical idea in Schopenhauer's philosophy – that nonexistence is preferable to life, that the goal of life should be the denial of the Will, which is tantamount to the extinction of the self.

Once we acknowledge the importance of the musical interruption at m. 55 of the second song, it is possible to approach the ensuing G major and E minor/major material (in no. 3) as something that lies beyond the normal flat-side tonal regions of the cycle. And, with that, we can hear the key of E♭ major in the last song as consistent with the material that precedes the interruption. With this in mind, I will skip over the third song for the moment and consider no. 4 as it relates to the interruption in mm. 55–57 of no. 2.

IV

The construction of the fourth song's text reinforces the emphasis on love that is already explicit in its content. To grasp this point we need to consider the whole of 1 Cor. 13:

> [1] If I speak in the tongues of mortals and of angels, but do not have love, I am a noisy gong or a clanging cymbal. [2] And if I have prophetic powers and understand all mysteries, and all knowledge, and I have all faith, so as to remove mountains, but do not have love, I am nothing. [3] If I give away all my possessions, and I hand over my body so that I may boast, but do not have love, I gain nothing.
>
> [4] Love is patient; love is kind; love is not envious or boastful or arrogant [5] or rude. It does not insist on its own way; it is not irritable or

14. Arnold Whittall, "The *Vier ernste Gesänge* Op. 121: Enrichment and Uniformity," in *Brahms*, 200.

resentful; [6] it does not rejoice in wrongdoing, but rejoices in the truth.
[7] It bears all things, believes all things, hopes all things, endures all
things.

[8] Love never ends. But as for prophecies, they will come to an end; as
for tongues, they will cease; as for knowledge, it will come to an end. [9]
For we know only in part, and we prophecy only in part; [10] but when the
complete comes, the partial will come to an end. [11] When I was a child,
I spoke like a child, I thought like a child, I reasoned like a child; when I
became an adult, I put an end to childish ways.

[12] For now we see in a mirror, dimly, but then we will see face to face.
Now I know only in part; then I will know fully, even as I have been fully
known. [13] And now, faith, hope, and love abide, these three; and the
greatest of these is love.

After comparing love with other spiritual gifts (vv. 1–3), Paul tells us
what love *is* and *is not* (vv. 4–7) and how it is superior to other spiritual
gifts (vv. 8–10). Verses 11–12 digress into the now-then completions,
before the first two words of v. 13 ("And now" ["Nun aber"]) suddenly
snap the reader back into the main theme of the chapter – love as a
spiritual gift. Verse 13 places a poignant accent on love, forcing the
reader to make a connection between love and the three completions.
Brahms sharpens the connection by omitting vv. 4–10 ("Love is patient; . . . the partial will come to an end"), thereby specifically juxtapos-
ing the comparisons of vv. 1–3 with the mirror metaphor. He also highlights the sudden change in discourse (from comparison to metaphor)
by moving abruptly from E♭ major to the distant key of B major in which
the mirror material is set (mm. 48–75). The return to E♭ major at m. 76
jolts the listener back to the tonal world of vv. 1–3, just as the words
"nun aber" in that measure return the listener to the theme of love.
Still, the mirror and its key (B major) remain a mystery.

The passage in B major would seem less mysterious had Brahms
spelled it in C♭. Indeed, the connecting transitional material in and out
of this section (mm. 47–48 and 75–76) refers to C♭ major as ♭III in E♭
major: m. 47 cadences on a G♭⁷ harmony, and m. 75 ends with a C♭⁷
harmony that is spelled as a German-sixth chord in E♭ major. Furthermore, Brahms had already introduced the final verse of the first section
in that key ("Und wenn ich alle meine Habe"; mm. 29ff.). But while C♭
major is a fairly unremarkable ♭III, B major suggests another tonal
world. The use of B major in no. 4 is no mere notational convenience:
that key recalls the mysterious B♮ that transfigured no. 2. And both

these sudden changes in harmonic direction stand out as problematic transition points in the cycle.

We may not easily perceive the B major of the mirror in no. 4 as a projection of the note B that turned away from nonexistence in m. 57 of no. 2. But therein lies the mystery: the image in the mirror is something "we see [i.e., hear] and yet cannot grasp." What we do hear is the sense of repose brought on by the slower tempo (*adagio*), the long-breathed phrases, and the relatively stable sense of key. Above all, perhaps, at the beginning and end of this section we hear for one of the few times in the cycle the voice moving in unison or above the uppermost notes of the accompaniment. By contrast, the words "und der noch nicht ist" in no. 2 had provided one of the few instances in the cycle when the voice joined with the *bass* line of the accompaniment.

The only overtly disruptive feature in mm. 48–75 of the fourth song is the pair of hemiolas that occur in the vocal part at the words "dann aber" (mm. 54–55 and 65–66), which form the syntactic center in each of the now-then completions. While these words point cognitively ahead, to some future "dann," their setting simultaneously looks back to the E♭-major arpeggios that set the words "Liebe nicht" in mm. 7–8 and 24–25 since these words likewise are set to prominent hemiolas. Each setting of "Liebe nicht" leads to a V^7/IV–IV cadence on A♭ major, the same harmony with which the song awkwardly began.

That opening harmony is quite surprising since it involves an enharmonic shift from the end of no. 3. When the piano enters with a *forte* A♭-major chord, only the high G♯ of the piano at the end of no. 3 ($\hat{3}$ in E major) remains, respelled as A♭ ($\hat{4}$ in E♭) and reversed from melody to bass note. This reversal of position symbolizes a complete reversal of musical direction, one that returns us to the flat-side key of E♭ major. The hemiolas on "Liebe nicht" comment on the harmonically unsettled material that surrounds them in mm. 1–47 and on the song's awkward entrance, as if to say, "Even if I move through all these keys, if I don't have love, I end up in the same unbalanced position in which I began!" Love, the music explains, is the key to landing on our feet.

While referring to these earlier hemiolas, the "dann aber" hemiolas in the second part of the song also point ahead to the final section (mm. 83–99), in which the B-major material returns in E♭ major. There, the same hemiola sets the word "Liebe," again on the subdominant (mm. 89–90), before reaching a convincing cadence on the tonic at m. 95. Love has indeed righted the unbalanced phrases of the song's first part, as foretold – in the mirror – by the "denn aber" hemiolas of mm. 54–55 and 65–66.

Everything is "completed" in the closing section, where the "mirror" material of mm. 48–75 is set in the tonic (so that we *can* grasp it); the voice returns to the middle of the accompaniment's range; and the piano finally partakes in the "love hemiolas" by rhythmically echoing them in mm. 91–92 and 95–96. E♭, which appeared to be a key of disruption at the beginning of the song, has become a key of synthesis by the end. And in mm. 95–97 the song is able to conclude with a gentle reversal of the fiery tonic E♭ arpeggio of m. 2, now rising to, rather than falling from, G. Finally, the elusive tonic is quietly but securely stated in the piano as, for the first time in the cycle, the voice ends on the tonic pitch. The end of the song returns not only to E♭ major but to love as well. Love is the synthesizing element that, when added to the incomplete image in the mirror, brings us to a state of completion, a whole.

V

What part, then, does no. 3 play in the cycle? This question stands the prevailing interpretation of the *Vier ernste Gesänge* on its head since the third song has the most to say about death in a cycle that is usually thought of as death oriented. "O Tod" does play a role in my interpretation, and it is one that draws us toward the important question of why Brahms chose the Bible as his textual source.

I have already noted that the text of the third song is balanced between two views of death ("bitter" and "sweet") and that this view lies close to the Lutheran view of death as a comforter. Moreover, I have argued that the acceptance of death implied by the text of no. 3 registers, not a continuation of Qoheleth's view of death in the first and second songs, but a step back from the nihilism there. If we hear the interruption in no. 2 as a reaction against something abhorrent, then we can assume that the ensuing tonal digression to sharp-side keys represents a retreat to something comfortable and familiar, specifically, to the traditional Lutheran way of dealing with death.

Arnold Schoenberg called no. 3 "the most touching of the whole cycle – in spite of its perfection, if not *because* of it."[15] That statement

15. Arnold Schoenberg, "Brahms the Progressive," in *Style and Idea*, ed. Leonard Stein (Berkeley: University of California Press, 1975), 439.

Example 7.5: Descending thirds in op. 121, no. 3: *a*, mm. 1–2;
b, mm. 19–20.

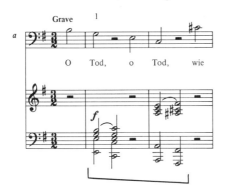

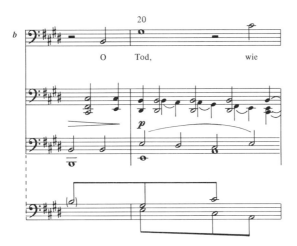

follows an analysis in which Schoenberg uncovers the permeation of the song's material by the interval of a third. A part of that permeation consists of the voice and accompaniment sharing the third, both as an abstract interval and in particular transpositions. Thus, Schoenberg demonstrates that the descent by thirds from B to F♯ in mm. 1–2 (and again in mm. 12–14) is shared across the voice and accompaniment: B–G–E–C in the voice and E–C–A–F♯ in the piano (ex. 7.5*a*). By the same token, in the beginning of the song's second half (mm. 19ff.), the first statement of "O Tod wie wohl tust du," in E major, can be heard as an extended chain of thirds, starting with the B–G♯ in the voice and the E–C♯–A in the piano (ex. 7.5*b*). Following Schoenberg's lead, we can come to a unified understanding of the song's two halves when we consider that their music, so outwardly different in affect, is derived

{187}

from the same substance. Such a complete integration of material accounts for the sense of balance and repose conveyed by "O Tod." It also provides a sense of musical equilibrium – perhaps the "perfection" to which Schoenberg referred – that is an appropriate expression of Lutheran comfort in death.

Why, if the solution to the problem posed by Qoheleth demanded going further, did Brahms turn to this source of comfort in the middle of his cycle? His reasons might be connected to Wagner's appropriation of Schopenhauer's philosophy. Brahms's concept of love differed sharply from the more radical one espoused by Wagner, although both had their roots in Romanticism. Love in op. 121 carries no Tristanesque relationship to death. Rather, it goes beyond death to overcome the nothingness, the "weltlösende Nacht der Liebe" of which Tristan and Isolde sing. Brahms, therefore, may have sensed that some expression of the more traditional view of death was necessary, lest the listener wrongly equate the love of no. 4 with the death of the first two songs. Setting *Tod* in the distant sharp-side keys of E minor and E major helps deter any such equation.

Whereas the legacy of Romanticism drew Wagner and his followers to the more *völkisch* realm of Christian myth and legend, it drew Brahms to Luther's Bible. The German Romantics highly prized the Bible and were deeply influenced by it: we have already seen evidence of that in the influence that Paul had on Hegel and Hölderlin.[16] It was only natural that Brahms would turn to the Bible for texts that would allow him to express his opposition to the pessimism of Schopenhauer. The *Vier ernste Gesänge* bear witness to a debate of divergent Romantic ideologies in the second half of the nineteenth century; they allow us to hear Paul's ideas, in Luther's words, as a rebuttal to the pessimism of Ecclesiastes and Schopenhauer. For Brahms, the final nothingness is superseded by the faith of the early Romantics in the divine power of love, and this is expressed in the "Gottvertrauende" words of Luther's Bible.

16. For a discussion of the Bible and the Romantics, see M. H. Abrams, *Natural Supernaturalism: Tradition and Revolution in Romantic Literature* (New York: W. W. Norton & Co., 1971).

CONTRIBUTORS

DANIEL BELLER-MCKENNA, who received his doctorate in musicology from Harvard University in 1994, is Assistant Professor of Music at the University of South Carolina. His essay on op. 121 is drawn from his dissertation, "Brahms, the Bible, and Post-Romanticism: Cultural Issues in Johannes Brahms's Later Settings of Biblical Texts, 1877–1896," for which he was awarded an AMS 50 Fellowship.

GEORGE S. BOZARTH, Associate Professor of Music at the University of Washington, served as director of the 1983 International Brahms Conference at the Library of Congress and editor of *Brahms Studies: Analytical and Historical Perspectives* (Oxford University Press). His articles on Brahms include studies on compositional process, problems in chronology, documents, and editorial issues. His critical edition of the organ works of Brahms (G. Henle Verlag) appeared in 1988, and his edition of the correspondence between Brahms and Robert Keller will soon be released by the University of Nebraska Press.

IRA BRAUS, who has taught at Bates College, has published widely in both historical and cognitive musicology. He is an accomplished pianist and is noted for his performances of the music of Brahms on a J. B. Streicher piano that was built within two years of the model used by the composer himself.

DAVID BRODBECK is Associate Professor of Music at the University of Pittsburgh. He has contributed essays to *Brahms Studies: Analytical and Historical Studies* (Oxford University Press), *Mendelssohn Studies* (Cambridge University Press), *Brahms and His World* and *Mendelssohn and His World* (both Princeton University Press), and *Schubert: Critical and Analytical Studies* (University of Nebraska Press), as well as to the periodicals *19th-Century Music* and *Journal of Musicology*. His current projects include an essay on Mendelssohn's choral music and a monograph on the Brahms symphonies.

JOHN DAVERIO is Associate Professor of Music and chair of the Musicology Department at Boston University. He is the author of *Nineteenth-Century Music and the German Romantic Ideology* (Schirmer Books) and has contributed articles on Schumann, Brahms, and Wagner to a number of periodicals, including *19th-Century Music, Journal of the American Musicology Society,* and *Journal of Musicology.* He is currently working on a study of the life and works of Robert Schumann.

JOSEPH DUBIEL is an associate professor in the Music Department of Columbia University. His vocal and chamber music has been performed throughout the United States, and he has published articles on many theoretical topics, including analytical methodology and twentieth-century music.

MARGARET NOTLEY received her doctorate from Yale University in 1992. Her research interests are centered on late nineteenth- and early twentieth-century Vienna, and her current work focuses on the politicization of the Viennese musical world in the 1880s and 1890s, which she has addressed in her recent "Brahms as Liberal: Genre, Style, and Politics in Late Nineteenth-Century Vienna" (*19th-Century Music*).

GENERAL INDEX

INDEX OF BRAHMS'S COMPOSITIONS